NEW HAMPSHIRE WILDLIFE VIEWING GUIDE

Judith K. Silverberg

FALCON™

HELENA, MONTANA

DEDICATION

. . . to those who see
   long lines of geese
       fade far beyond
           and know they come back again to nest
to those who see
   with wonder in their heart—
   and know—what glories there can be . . .

   Gwen Frostic

This guide is dedicated to those who listen in the early morning
hours, smell the earth, and marvel at wild and beautiful things.

ACKNOWLEDGMENTS

This guide became a reality because of the perseverance of the New Hampshire Wildlife Watching Program steering committee. The group believed in the project and its importance to people who value wildlife in ways only their hearts understand. I would like to thank the members of the steering committee for their support, encouragement, and vision. They represented a diverse group of agencies and organizations: the Audubon Society of New Hampshire, the Society for the Protection of New Hampshire Forests, the Beaver Brook Association, the Department of Resources and Economic Development, the U.S. Fish and Wildlife Service, the U.S. Forest Service, and the New Hampshire Fish and Game Department.

I would especially like to thank my colleagues from New Hampshire Fish and Game—Ed Robinson, John Kanter, John Lanier, and Judy Stokes—who spent extra time making this guide the best it could be. A special thank you to Paul Doscher, Tom Miner, Kathy Fair, and Steve Walker for coordinating efforts on behalf of their organizations and agencies.

The wildlife viewing program is about partnerships, and this guide would not have been complete without the efforts of Steve Barba from The BALSAMS, Don Merski from Boise Cascade, and Allan Peterson from Champion International Corporation.

I do not know how to express my thanks to Victor Young for producing the artwork that graces these pages. The New Hampshire Fish and Game Department is exceedingly lucky to have him as an employee.

Many others contributed to this project with site nominations, reviews of site descriptions, and countless important details. Still others, too numerous to list, kindly offered their knowledge of wildlife and of the relationships between wildlife and habitat.

And I would like to thank my family—my husband, Rick, and my children, Sarah and Beth—for sharing in this project and making the visits to the sites pleasurable and memorable. Finally I would like to thank my parents for instilling in me the ability to see.

Author and State Project Leader:
Judith K. Silverberg

Viewing Guide Program Manager:
Kate Davies, Defenders of Wildlife

Original Illustrations:
Victor E. Young

Front Cover Photo:
Moose calf by Charles H. Willey

Back Cover Photos:
Bald eagle by Charles H. Willey
Snowshoe hare by Tom and Pat Leeson

CONTENTS

REGION 3: SOUTHERN NEW HAMPSHIRE COASTAL PLAIN AND HILLS

SPONSORS

 The NEW HAMPSHIRE FISH AND GAME DEPARTMENT is guardian of New Hampshire's fish, wildlife, and marine resources. Working in partnership with the public, the Department conserves, manages, and protects these resources and their habitats, and informs, educates, and provides opportunities for the public to use and appreciate the resources. To learn more about the Fish and Game Department, contact us at 2 Hazen Drive, Concord, NH 03301, (603) 271-3211.

 DEFENDERS OF WILDLIFE is a national nonprofit organization of more than 100,000 members and supporters dedicated to preserving the natural abundance and diversity of wildlife and its habitat. A one-year membership is $20 and includes a subscription to *Defenders*, an award-winning conservation magazine. To join, or for further information, write or call Defenders of Wildlife, 1101 Fourteenth Street NW, Washington, DC 20005, (202) 682-9400.

  The NEW HAMPSHIRE DEPARTMENT OF RESOURCES AND ECONOMIC DEVELOPMENT manages 178,000 acres of public land through its Division of Parks and Recreation and Division of Forests and Lands. The Division of Parks and Recreation manages more than seventy state parks, historic sites, and recreation areas. Its mission is to preserve and protect New Hampshire's natural and cultural resources and to provide recreational and educational opportunities for New Hampshire residents and visitors. The 117 state forests managed by the Division of Forests and Lands provide areas for recreation, habitat for fish and wildlife, abundant water supplies, and growth areas for timber. For information, contact the New Hampshire Division of Parks and Recreation, P.O. Box 1856, Concord, NH 03302, (603) 271-3556; or the New Hampshire Division of Forests and Lands, P.O. Box 1856, Concord, NH 03302, (603) 271-3456.

 The USDA FOREST SERVICE is responsible for managing National Forest lands and their resources, and for protecting and restoring these lands to best serve the needs of the American people. The White Mountain National Forest in New Hampshire sponsors programs to promote awareness and enjoyment of fish and wildlife on public lands. Contact the White Mountain National Forest at P.O. Box 638, Laconia, NH 03247, (603) 524-6450.

 The U.S. FISH AND WILDLIFE SERVICE is pleased to support this project in furtherance of its mission to conserve, protect, and enhance fish and wildlife resources and their habitats. In New Hampshire, the Service manages the Great Bay, Lake Umbagog, and the Silvio O. Conte and John Hay National Wildlife Refuges. It is active in wetland protection and restoration, and in enforcement of federal fish and wildlife laws. Contact the US Fish and Wildlife Service at 22 Bridge Street, Concord, NH, 03301 (603) 225-1411.

BOISE CASCADE CORPORATION is an integrated paper and forest products company headquartered in Boise, Idaho. The company manufactures and distributes paper, office products, **Boise Cascade** and building materials, and owns and manages timberland to support these operations.

The DEPARTMENT OF DEFENSE is the steward of about 25 million acres of land in the United States, many of which possess irreplaceable natural and cultural resources. The DOD is pleased to support the National Watchable Wildlife Program through its Legacy Resource Management Program, a special initiative to enhance the conservation and restoration of natural and cultural resources on military land. For more information contact ODUSD (ES) EQ-LP, 3400 Defense Pentagon, Room 3E791, Arlington, VA 20301-3400.

Other important cooperators and contributors include: the Audubon Society of New Hampshire, the Society for the Protection of New Hampshire Forests, the Beaver Brook Association, The BALSAMS, Brick Mill Studios, Inc., and Champion International Corporation.

Copyright ©1997 by Falcon Press® Publishing Co., Inc., Helena and Billings, Montana.

Published in cooperation with Defenders of Wildlife.

All rights reserved, including the right to reproduce this book or any part thereof in any form, except brief quotations for reviews, without written permission of the publisher.

Design, typesetting, and other prepress work by Falcon Press®, Helena, Montana.

Printed in Korea.

Defenders of Wildlife and its design are registered marks of Defenders of Wildlife, Washington, D.C.

Watchable Wildlife® is a registered trademark of Falcon Press® Publishing Co., Inc.

All artwork Copyright© by the New Hampshire Fish and Game Department. All rights reserved.

Library of Congress Cataloging-in-Publication Data

Silverberg, Judith K. 1952-

New Hampshire wildlife viewing guide / Judith K. Silverberg.

p. cm.

Includes index.

ISBN 1-56044-544-0

1. Wildlife viewing sites—New Hampshire—Guidebooks. 2. Wildlife watching—New Hampshire—Guidebooks. 3. New Hampshire—Guidebooks.

I. Title.

QL192.S54 1997

333.95'4'09742—dc21

96-37280

CIP

INTRODUCTION

Every day is a good day for viewing wildlife, whether in your own backyard, a neighborhood park, or a new place you are exploring. In New Hampshire this is especially true: it is possible to see a moose in a front yard in Concord or hear a Bicknell's thrush in the higher elevations of Dixville Notch. From Mount Washington, where the worst weather in the world has been recorded, to the 18 miles of ocean coastline (dwarfed by the two-hundred-mile coastline of the Great Bay estuary), New Hampshire's landscape exhibits a diversity that few other places can match. More than 450 species of fish, mammals, birds, amphibians, and reptiles, as well as countless insects and marine animals, are part of our wildlife heritage.

More than 80 percent of New Hampshire is forested; this makes wildlife viewing somewhat challenging. Animals can easily remain hidden, allowing viewers only a glimpse as the animals turn and blend into their surroundings. Increasing your knowledge about what animals live where, and knowing at what season of the year species are most visible, will help you have successful viewing experiences. Listen in April and May for the choruses of spring peepers and wood frogs; they sing from the wetlands, trying to attract a mate. Early June is a good time to see bears grazing on the ski slopes of Cannon Mountain. Ospreys fly along the Androscoggin River in July and August. On a crisp, clear day in mid-September, Mount Kearsarge affords views of hundreds of broad-winged hawks as they migrate south. Winter is a great time to search for bald eagles along the lower Merrimack River in Manchester or to read the stories of winter survival by looking for tracks in the snow.

Choosing the 73 sites in this guide was a difficult task. More than 120 sites were suggested by people who know where to look for wildlife. Stringent criteria were used to select sites: among other things, successful sites had to have public access, allow for viewing without harming the resources, and offer the potential to see wildlife during at least one season of the year. All areas offer unique opportunities for learning more about the natural world.

This guide was designed for both the casual observer and the serious wildlife watcher; it offers a range of opportunities, from roadside sites to those requiring a two- to three-mile hike. About one-third of the sites have interpretive signs or brochures supplying natural history information to make your visit more interesting and enjoyable.

New Hampshire is home to some of the oldest conservation organizations in the United States and to the first National Forest. Our 20th century traditions of land stewardship have allowed many special places to remain. Public land and wildlife management agencies, private organizations, and businesses are working in partnership to ensure healthy wildlife populations for the future. Their work is supported by people like yourself who have an appreciation and understanding of the natural systems and diversity of wildlife surrounding us. So, whether you experience the excitement of watching a peregrine falcon diving from a building in downtown Manchester, marvel at the sound of coyotes howling on a moonlit night, or feel awe at the sight of the morning mist rising from a bog, know you are partaking of the essence of this place called New Hampshire.

THE NATIONAL WATCHABLE WILDLIFE PROGRAM

The National Watchable Wildlife Program is a nationwide cooperative effort to combine wildlife conservation with America's deepening interest in wildlife-related outdoor recreation. Since the 1970s, wildlife viewing has grown to be one of the most popular outdoor recreation activities.

For many years, hunters and anglers have supplied most of the funding for wildlife conservation by paying license fees and taxes on firearms and fishing tackle. These dollars funded public fish and wildlife areas, refuges, preserves, and management programs, all of which benefited all wildlife whether or not they were hunted. Though hunting in New Hampshire remains a strong tradition, national trends indicate that participation is dropping. This change has generated concern about the future source of wildlife conservation and recreation money. Efforts are underway at state and national levels to develop new funding mechanisms. The Watchable Wildlife Program is founded on the premise that people who enjoy and learn about wildlife in a natural setting will become advocates for conservation in the future.

The National Watchable Wildlife Program began in 1990 with the signing of a Memorandum of Understanding by eight federal land management agencies, the International Association of Fish and Wildlife Agencies, and four national conservation groups. Defenders of Wildlife assumed the role of nationwide program coordinator. The cornerstone of this program is the Watchable Wildlife Series of state-by-state wildlife viewing guides. The *New Hampshire Wildlife Viewing Guide* is the 25th guide in the series. Each of the sites mentioned in this book is marked with the brown and white binocular logo. Similar viewing networks have been established in over half the fifty states. Thus, the effort is part of a growing nationwide network.

The partnerships formed to produce the New Hampshire guide and viewing network will continue to work together on site development, interpretation, and conservation education. Some viewing sites will be enhanced with interpretive signs, trails, boardwalks, or viewing platforms. In addition, opportunities to participate in wildlife viewing programs will be available in the future.

Use this guide to plan outings that coincide with peak wildlife viewing periods. Consult it for interesting side trips while traveling. Take advantage of on-site education programs. Become an active partner in resource stewardship. We must work together to preserve healthy habitats and wildlife populations for our enjoyment as well as for the pleasure and well-being of future generations.

BIODIVERSITY

Biodiversity—short for biological diversity—is a big word for a simple concept: the variety of life in all its forms and the natural processes that maintain it. Scientists recognize four levels of biodiversity: genes, species, natural communities, and landscapes. New Hampshire offers many examples at each level, from dwarf wedge mussels and peregrine falcons to northern hardwood forests and pine barrens.

To understand the dynamic nature of biodiversity, we must focus on ecosystems and landscapes rather than on individual species. This larger view encompasses the full complexity of natural systems—the ecological, evolutionary, physical, and human processes that affect and sustain life.

Biological diversity benefits us in many ways. It is an economic resource, a reservoir of materials for use in medicine, agriculture, and industry. Worldwide, people use tens of thousands of plants and animals. Most medicines in use today originated from studies of wild species. The link between biodiversity and human health is clear. The diversity of living things performs a variety of services for us, including pollinating fruit and vegetable crops and controlling pests, at no cost to human society. In addition, the plants and animals found in this country appeal to tourists and others who come here to enjoy the outdoors.

As part of the biological community, humans depend on natural systems for survival. Living organisms enrich the soil that grows our food; they generate the oxygen we breathe. Earth's systems function because of the diversity of life forms and the interactions between these life forms. The reasons for maintaining biodiversity are varied and often difficult to quantify, yet all contribute to a greater quality of life.

Humans have lived in New Hampshire for a thousand or more years. As populations have grown, the effects of human habits on the natural environment have also grown. In the last two hundred years, at least six species of mammals and birds that once inhabited New Hampshire and its adjacent waters have disappeared forever: the Labrador duck, the sea mink, the great auk, the passenger pigeon, the heath hen, and the scrag whale.

In the future, our challenge will be to conserve the resources we have through living more compatibly with our natural environment. People are as much a component of the ecosystem as plants and animals.

TOOLS AND TECHNIQUES FOR WILDLIFE VIEWING

There is nothing quite as exciting as seeing animals in the wild. You can never be sure what you will see; this helps make watching wildlife a rewarding experience. Watching wildlife can be a goal in itself or it can be an added benefit on a fishing trip, a hike, or any outing. There are a number of things you can do to increase your chances of seeing wildlife.

Binoculars. These are among the most helpful of a wildlife watcher's tools. Selecting a good pair can be complicated; learn all you can before you buy. The best all-purpose binoculars are those with a magnification power of 7 and a lens diameter of 35. A pair of 7x35 binoculars gathers a lot of light, making them useful for morning and evening viewing. Locate the animal with the naked eye first. Then, without shifting your gaze, bring the binoculars to your eyes and focus.

Clothing. Dressing in layers allows you to adjust to changing weather. The time of year will determine how many layers you need. The color of your clothes may affect what animals you see. Birds can see color well. It is best to wear drab, earthy colors to help avoid detection.

Field Guides. Use field guides, checklists, and other resources to identify wildlife and learn about animal habits and habitats. These materials can open up a world of information to enrich your experience.

Go Out When Wildlife Is Active. Plan your visit around peak viewing seasons or times of activity. New Hampshire boasts several activity peaks. The first is April through June, when large numbers of migratory birds return and animals are busy raising their young. A second peak occurs in September and October as migratory birds begin to head south and mammals prepare for winter. The time of day also plays an important part in whether or not you will see animals. In general, wildlife is more active during the first and last hours of daylight.

Be Patient, Learn to Be Still and Silent. You can improve your chances of seeing wildlife by slowing down. Take a few steps, stop, listen, and look. Sharpen your senses by paying attention to sounds and smells. Look for changes in shapes and in movement all around you. Avoid making noise: don't step on brittle sticks and leaves or talk out loud. If possible, walk into the wind. If you arrive at a wildlife viewing site expecting to see a lot of wildlife right away, you will probably be disappointed. Allow yourself time. In some cases, you can blend into your surroundings by sitting motionless next to a tree or bush, and the wildlife in the area will more likely go about their daily routines.

Use a Blind. If you can conceal yourself, you'll increase your chances of having a successful viewing experience. Simply standing behind a tree or bush instead of out in the open can help. Cars, boats, and canoes make excellent viewing blinds. Animals are often used to seeing these things and may not feel threatened or disturbed unless you try to get out.

Prepare for Your Outing. Some of the viewing sites in this guide are remote; some have no facilities. Review the site account before you set out, checking for warnings about road conditions and weather. If it is a site you are hiking into, make sure you know where you are going and have water, proper footgear, and appropriate clothing. Expect to encounter insects in spring and summer; bring along repellents and wear protective clothing. A hat with a brim and good sunglasses can protect your eyes from the sun; use sunblock to protect your skin.

VIEWING ETHICS AND RESPONSIBILITIES

Most people who spend time outdoors care a great deal about wildlife and wildlife habitat. However, even the innocent act of observing wildlife, if not performed properly, can have a great impact on animals. Following a few guidelines will help put the needs and safety of wildlife first, conserve wildlife and habitats, and respect the rights of others.

Enjoy Wildlife from a Distance. The goal of successful wildlife watching is to see animals without interrupting their normal behavior. An animal sends clear signals if you come too close: it stops feeding and raises its head sharply, moves away, changes direction of travel, or appears nervous or aggressive. Any disturbance may result in an animal abandoning its young, injuring itself as it tries to escape, not feeding at a time of critical energy need, or displaying aggressive behavior toward the intruder.

Don't Feed the Animals. While it may seem exciting at the time to have an animal eat out of your hand, the potential consequences are serious. Some animals become accustomed to handouts and lose their natural fear of humans. They may become aggressive with visitors who refuse to feed them. If human injury results, so, usually, does the death of the animal involved. Human food does not meet the nutritional requirements of many animals, and it may seriously harm them. Animals that become accustomed to handouts may be faced with starvation when the food source disappears.

Never Chase or Harass Animals. In some cases, pursuing animals forces them to use up valuable energy resources needed for survival. Make sure to leave pets at home; your viewing experience will be more successful as well as more comfortable for the wildlife.

Don't Pick Up Orphaned or Sick Animals. Wild animals rarely abandon their young. In most cases, the adults are nearby, waiting for visitors to leave before returning to their young. If an animal appears sick or injured, behaves oddly, or seems tame, leave it alone. A number of wildlife diseases (including rabies) can affect humans.

Honor the Rights of Private Landowners and Fellow Recreationists. Always ask permission before entering private property and leave no trace that you have been there. Respect the rights of other viewers at a site. Be considerate when approaching wildlife that is already being viewed; a loud noise or quick movement may spoil the experience for everyone. Remember, you share the woods with many other recreationists, including hikers, snowmobilers, mountain bikers, and hunters. Most public lands are open to hunting and fishing. Information on hunting season dates and regulations is available from the Public Affairs Division of the New Hampshire Fish and Game Department as well as from license agents.

PHOTO TIPS

1. For general wildlife photography, use medium-speed slide films such as ASA (ISO) 100 Fujichrome or Ektachrome, or ASA (ISO) 64 Kodachrome. In print film, use ASA (ISO) 100 or 200.

2. Slower-speed film is better for landscape and scenic shots. Use films such as Kodachrome 25, Velvia Fujichrome ASA (ISO) 50, or Ektachrome 50HC. Kodak's Ektar ASA (ISO) 25 print film is great for enlargements.

3. Early morning and late afternoon are the best times to photograph.

4. A wide-angle lens (20 to 28 mm) can capture scenic shots. Use the greatest depth of field possible.

5. A telephoto (200 to 400 mm) lens is best for closeups of wildlife. Make sure to give enough space to the animal being photographed so it will behave more naturally.

6. For sharp pictures, use a tripod. Consider using a tripod and shutter cable release for shooting in early-morning or late-evening light.

7. Do not leave your film or camera in a closed vehicle in hot weather.

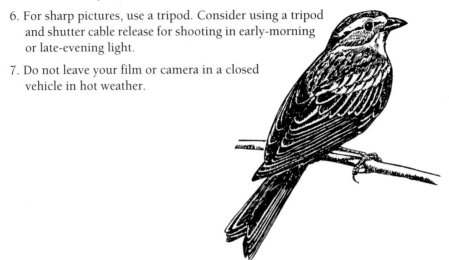

WINTER WILDLIFE VIEWING

Winter provides a challenging opportunity to view wildlife. Winter's snows help provide clues to the lives of wild creatures. In winter you can find where a grouse spent a night in the snow or discover tracks of a fisher close to your house. The records wildlife leaves behind are our link to how they behave and survive. Learning about tracks, scat, and other signs left by wildlife can give us insight into their secret world.

Winter poses challenges to the natural world. Many of the birds we see in the summer migrate to find food and escape the cold. Woodland jumping mice and woodchucks hibernate, lowering their respiration rates and body temperature. When the weather is most severe, many mammals will find shelter and sleep through the worst of it.

Snow is a mixed blessing for animals. Voles, shrews, and mice remain active throughout the winter, using the snow to protect them from predators, shelter them from winds, and insulate them from cold temperatures. Deep snow may allow rabbits and snowshoe hares to nibble buds and ends of twigs which would otherwise be above their reach. On the other hand, deeper snow hinders deer as they run, making them more vulnerable to predators and causing them to use more energy in their search for food.

Some animals have adapted to walking on snow. For example, snowshoe hares grow extra fur on their feet and grouse develop comb-like fringes along the edges of their toes. Animals like the snowshoe hare and ermine change color in winter to blend in with the white environment.

Tracks, Tracks, and More Tracks: The most common wildlife sign we see are tracks in the snow. By following tracks we can tell what direction an animal was going, if it was alone, and what it was doing. Because snow conditions are so variable, you may never see a clear print that matches a picture in a field guide. But if you can identify the five basic modes of travel and the pattern they leave behind you will have a clue as to who was there: 1. Pacing—both legs on the right side move and then both legs on the left side move. 2. Diagonal walking—the front leg on the right and the back leg on the left move, then the front leg on the left and the back leg on the right move. 3. Trotting—similar to the diagonal walk except the whole body is lifted off the ground at some point. 4. Bounding—the front feet reach out together and then the hind feet follow as a pair. 5. Galloping—the hind feet land in front of the front feet. Other clues needed to identify the track include size and distance between tracks.

Hints for Following Tracks: Tracks can be found anywhere, but they are often most common where two habitats meet, such as along the edge between a wetland and a forest. Walk alongside a track so you can look back and get a sense for the pattern. Bring along a pocket track card with a ruler so you can identify clear prints and be able to make measurements. Follow the track for a while to see if the pattern or direction changes. For example, if you are following a galloping track pattern and it ends at a tree, depending upon the track size you will know if it is a mouse or a squirrel.

Look for Other Wildlife Sign: Besides tracks, look for stray feathers, a drop of blood, scat, and urine markings. These can provide more clues about what animal made the track. Look for evidence of where wildlife has been feeding. Are the red maple twigs cut off on a sharp, almost 45-degree angle? Or are they gnawed off? The former tells us that a rabbit or snowshoe hare has been feeding. The latter tells us it must have been a deer or moose. This kind of information will allow us to narrow the possibilities. Gnawed bark, tree dens, holes in the ice, and turned-over rotten logs are all evidence of wildlife.

Birds in Winter: There are approximately 60 kinds of land birds that can be commonly found in New Hampshire in the winter. Many of these birds are easily attracted to bird feeders. Black-capped chickadees, white- and red-breasted nuthatches, American goldfinches, evening grosbeaks, blue jays, and others provide many bird watchers with countless hours of joy. If you are looking for these birds in places other than at feeders, scan the limbs and trunks of trees and you will likely see them. Or you might see brown creepers and downy and hairy woodpeckers. Since February is mating time for barred, great horned, screech, and saw-whet owls, a cold, crisp night is an ideal time to listen for and locate them.

Winter is a good time to view waterfowl on Great Bay and on rivers and lakes that don't freeze. It also possible to sight bald eagles along the Merrimack River and on Great Bay.

Prepare Yourself: Since we are not adapted to living constantly in the cold, it is important we remember a few key things when viewing wildlife in the winter.

- Dress in layers, so you can regulate your body temperature and be neither too hot nor too cold.
- Under your roomy boots wear a thin and a thick pair of socks.
- Since a tremendous amount of heat is lost through your head, wear a warm hat.
- Mittens are better than gloves for keeping your hands warm. Try a light weight glove inside a mitten so if you need to adjust your binoculars, snow shoes, or camera you can do it without exposing your hand to the cold.
- Always let someone know where you are going and never travel alone.
- Water is as important in the winter as it is in the summer.
- Always carry food with you to give you extra energy and warmth.
- Your wildlife viewing pack should include a map and a compass as well as a flashlight or headlamp. Remember, batteries do not last very long when it is cold.
- Plan your explorations to be out of the woods before dark.
- If there are more than a couple of inches of snow on the ground you are going to want to have snowshoes or cross-country skis, especially if you are going to go off a trail. All your equipment should be in good condition and properly adjusted before setting out on a trek.

Winter Wildlife Viewing Ethics: In winter it is even more important to enjoy wildlife from a distance. This is a time of critical energy needs for all wildlife. If you approach too closely and cause an animal to change its behavior, it may mean the difference between life and death for that animal. It is best to stay out of places like moose and deer yards, where your mere presence raises heart rates and may stimulate the need to use precious energy.

Where to View Wildlife in Winter: One of the best places to look for wildlife in winter may be your own backyard. Many of the viewing sites listed in this book are accessible in winter, although parking may be limited. Keep in mind that the kinds and abundance of wildlife you see will be different from those found during the spring, summer, and fall.

VIEWING MOOSE

So far, New Hampshire has been fortunate that no one has been hurt while viewing moose. Residents and nonresidents alike often forget moose are large, unpredictable, wild animals. It's not unusual to see cars stopped in the middle of the road with Mom, Dad, and the kids piling out to get a closer look with no regard for themselves or the moose. Parents who are normally very protective will even put their children in front of a moose to get a cute picture.

Moose are large animals, averaging 1,000 pounds and standing six feet at the shoulder. While they have poor eyesight, their senses of smelling and hearing are excellent. Equipped with four strong legs and sharp hooves, they are capable of moving at speeds up to 40 miles an hour. Bulls have antlers with multiple sharp points that can be used as protection. Unlike deer, moose do not have an automatic flight response. Moose don't have to run away—they are the largest thing around.

An adult moose has little to fear from predators. It takes a whole pack of wolves to kill a healthy adult moose, and even then the wolves are only successful one out of ten times. In New Hampshire, moose don't have to worry about wolves. Moose are vulnerable only to accidents and to hunters during a limited hunting season.

Because moose don't flee like other wild animals, they often get labeled as stupid or tame. Don't be fooled—they are neither. Alway view moose from a distance. Be especially careful to give females and their calves plenty of room. Like any wild animal, a female moose will do anything to protect her young from a perceived threat.

Moose in the middle of the road are a frequent sight in the North Country from late spring through fall. Slow down and be alert when driving in moose country.
CHARLES H. WILLEY

From the time the snow leaves the ground to the early fall, it is almost guaranteed you can see a moose or several moose in areas where road salt accumulates. These boggy, wet areas along the sides of the road where the moose have churned up the mud are referred to as licks. In this situation, moose quickly learn that people are not a threat, and people can get closer than they would in any other situation. This kind of behavior is referred to as habituation; the animal tolerates your presence. Each individual moose has a different level of tolerance. In many cases, a moose will disappear in the darkness and shadows of the adjoining forest when people get too close, or it will bolt out across the road. You never know when or how a moose will react. It may even run down the source of the perceived threat and stomp on it.

Poor eyesight explains some other behaviors. If a moose doesn't smell or hear you, it may approach for a closer look. This often occurs when a moose is in the woods, a backyard, or a city. Usually the moose will trot off in the other direction when it realizes you are a human. Young animals may approach even closer before they react.

During the fall breeding season, young bulls will be driven off by both older bulls and cows. This causes the youngsters to travel great distances in search of a mate, often showing up in cities and on farms. Bulls are extremely aggressive during the breeding season and should be enjoyed from a long, safe distance.

There is no doubt watching moose is fun and exciting. They often tolerate us, but that doesn't mean they are tame. It is up to us to make sure we view moose responsibly.

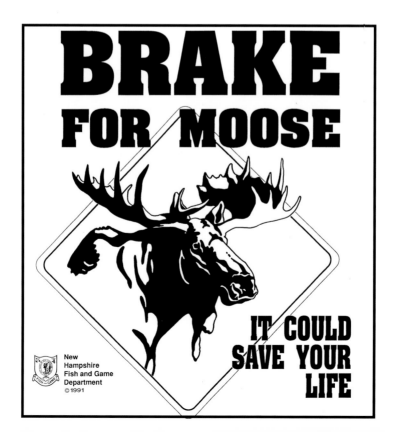

Follow these basic rules:

1- Keep your distance.
2- Use your car as a viewing blind. If you pull your car off the road, make sure it is off the traveled part of the highway and that it can be seen.
3- Never underestimate the speed with which a moose can react.
4- Watch quietly and do not disturb the animals' normal behavior.
5- Respect a moose's size and power.

By using common sense and following the above guidelines you will have a safe wildlife viewing experience that can provide you wonderful memories for a lifetime. Adapted from an article appearing in the *New Hampshire Wildlife Journal* © 1996.

HOW TO USE THIS GUIDE

This guide is divided into three sections, representing the principal biophysical regions of New Hampshire. At the beginning of each section, wildlife viewing sites are listed and located on a map. The text for each viewing site includes the following elements, which describe and interpret the habitats and the wildlife you may see. Pay attention to NOTES OF CAUTION in capital letters.

Description: Briefly explains the area, facilities, and wildlife.

Viewing Information: Expands on the site description, providing the seasonal likelihood of spotting wildlife along with other interesting information about the area. May include details about access and parking.

Directions: *Provides written directions for each site. Supplement this information with an up-to-date New Hampshire road map or a New Hampshire Atlas and Gazetteer.*

Ownership: Includes the name of the agency, organization, or company that owns or manages the site. The telephone number listed may be used to obtain more information.

Recreation and Facility Icons: Indicates some of the facilities and opportunities available at each site. The managing agency or organization can provide more information and describe other types of opportunities available.

 Parking
 Entry Fee or Use Fee
 Restrooms
 Barrier-Free
 Picnic
 Snowmobiling
 Fishing
 Camping

 Hiking Trails
 Cross-Country Skiing
 Bicycling
 Boat Ramp
 Motorized Boats
 Non-motorized Boats
 Horse Trails
Hunting

Site Owner/Manager Abbreviations
NHFG—New Hampshire Fish and Game Department
DRED—Department of Resources and Economic Development,
Division of Parks and Recreation and Division of Forests and Lands
USFS—United States Forest Service (White Mountain National Forest)
USFWS—United States Fish and Wildlife Service
USACE—United States Army Corps of Engineers
ASNH—Audubon Society of New Hampshire
SPNHF—Society for the Protection of New Hampshire Forests
PSNH—Public Service of New Hampshire
GBNERR—Great Bay National Estuarine Research Reserve

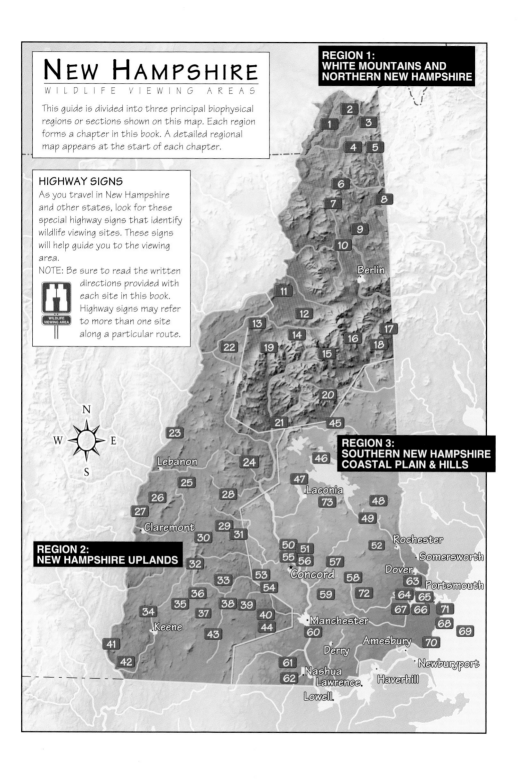

NEW HAMPSHIRE
WILDLIFE VIEWING AREAS

This guide is divided into three principal biophysical regions or sections shown on this map. Each region forms a chapter in this book. A detailed regional map appears at the start of each chapter.

HIGHWAY SIGNS

As you travel in New Hampshire and other states, look for these special highway signs that identify wildlife viewing sites. These signs will help guide you to the viewing area.

NOTE: Be sure to read the written directions provided with each site in this book. Highway signs may refer to more than one site along a particular route.

REGION 1:
WHITE MOUNTAINS AND
NORTHERN NEW HAMPSHIRE

Berlin

REGION 3:
SOUTHERN NEW HAMPSHIRE
COASTAL PLAIN & HILLS

Lebanon

Laconia

Rochester

Somersworth

Claremont

REGION 2:
NEW HAMPSHIRE UPLANDS

Concord

Dover

Portsmouth

Keene

Manchester

Amesbury

Derry

Newburyport

Nashua
Lawrence   Haverhill
Lowell

N
W   E
S

21

REGION 1—WHITE MOUNTAINS AND NORTHERN NEW HAMPSHIRE

From the high elevations of the White Mountains to the hilly lake country of the northern border, this is the northwoods of New Hampshire. In winter, snow-covered peaks and evergreen spires create a place of breathtaking beauty. People come from all over the world to experience the colors of autumn. The land is dominated by forests, though farms nestle in the major river valleys.

Sugar maple, yellow birch, American beech, red spruce, and balsam fir grow in abundance. Farther north as well as higher in elevation, boreal forest takes over. The higher peaks enter the alpine zone, where you are taller than anything around you. Some of the plants here are the same as those found in the Canadian arctic, while others, such as Robbins cinquefoil, occur only here.

Typical wildlife of this region includes moose, bears, fishers, and snowshoe hares. Dark-eyed juncos, evening grosbeaks, and boreal chickadees live here year-round. Common loons, ospreys, and Blackburnian and bay-breasted warblers are among the summer residents.

In addition to providing opportunities to view wildlife, the Kancamagus Highway affords spectacular views of the White Mountains. The landscape is dominated by red spruce, balsam fir, sugar maple, yellow birch, and American beech.
GEORGE WUERTHNER

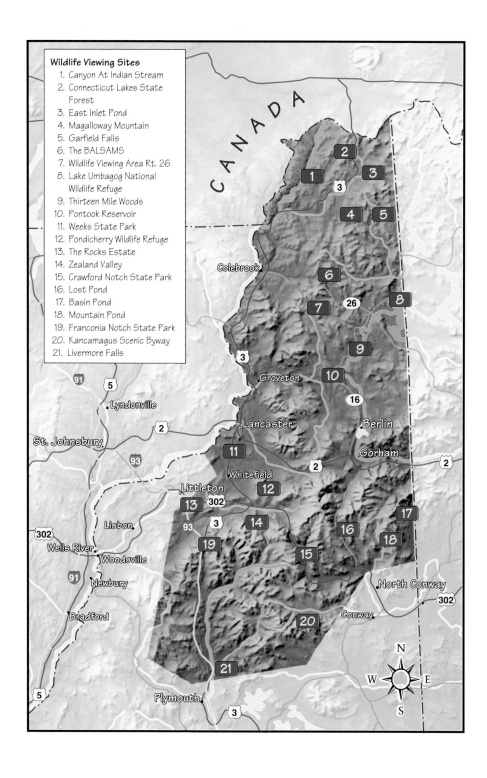

Wildlife Viewing Sites
1. Canyon At Indian Stream
2. Connecticut Lakes State Forest
3. East Inlet Pond
4. Magalloway Mountain
5. Garfield Falls
6. The BALSAMS
7. Wildlife Viewing Area Rt. 26
8. Lake Umbagog National Wildlife Refuge
9. Thirteen Mile Woods
10. Pontook Reservoir
11. Weeks State Park
12. Pondicherry Wildlife Refuge
13. The Rocks Estate
14. Zealand Valley
15. Crawford Notch State Park
16. Lost Pond
17. Basin Pond
18. Mountain Pond
19. Franconia Notch State Park
20. Kancamagus Scenic Byway
21. Livermore Falls

CANADA

Colebrook

Groveton

Lyndonville

Lancaster

Berlin

St. Johnsbury

Gorham

Whitefield

Littleton

Lisbon

Wells River

Woodsville

Newbury

North Conway

Bradford

Conway

Plymouth

N
W E
S

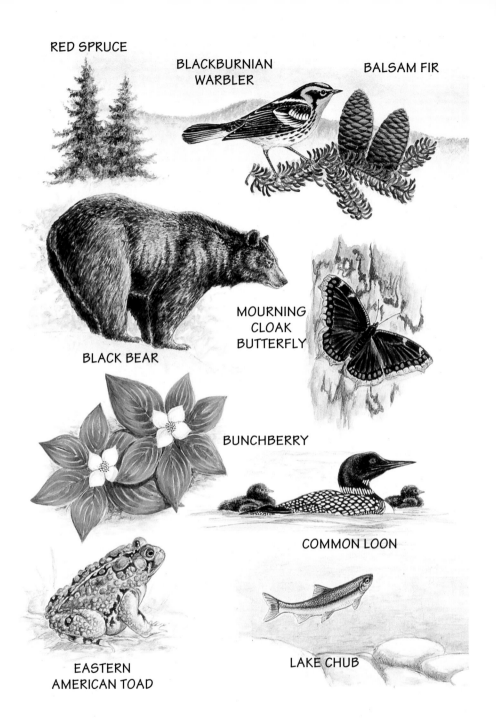

RED SPRUCE

BLACKBURNIAN
WARBLER

BALSAM FIR

BLACK BEAR

MOURNING
CLOAK
BUTTERFLY

BUNCHBERRY

COMMON LOON

EASTERN
AMERICAN TOAD

LAKE CHUB

Northern New Hampshire
In areas of this region where the soil is better and the climate even only slightly
moderated, spruce-fir forest gives way to northern hardwoods. Birch, beech, and
maple are the deciduous trees that dominate the area. This is the place to look for

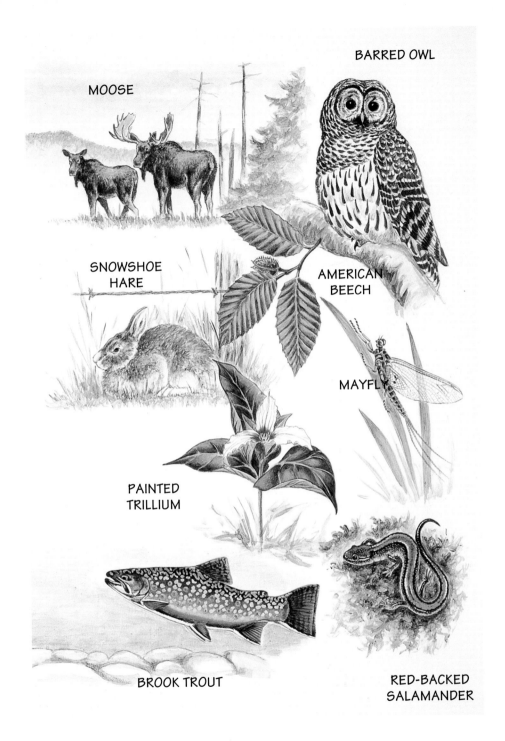

MOOSE

BARRED OWL

SNOWSHOE HARE

AMERICAN BEECH

MAYFLY

PAINTED TRILLIUM

BROOK TROUT

RED-BACKED SALAMANDER

color, from the wildflowers of early spring to the brilliant fall displays of reds and golds to the dark shades of evergreens. Snowshoe hares, barred owls, and moose use their adaptations to survive the winter snows. Colorful warblers, like the Blackburnian, fill the air with song on a spring morning.

Description: Located in a remote part of a working forest, this beautiful half-mile canyon is carved through layers of solid rock. The streambed has many kettle holes—holes that are formed when a small stone is caught and held in a depression by rushing water. Over time, the twirling stone creates a smooth pocket in the rock. Northern hardwoods, red spruce, and balsam fir climb the steep banks. The canyon is a fifty-acre "Special Place in the Forest" owned by Champion. A well-marked trail leads you from the parking area to the canyon. *BE CAREFUL—THE CANYON HAS STEEP DROP-OFFS AND SLIPPERY FOOTING.*

Viewing Information: A variety of wildlife uses this setting, including moose, foxes, coyotes, and deer. Bird life is abundant in the summer; look for boreal chickadees, purple finches, and winter wrens. Listen carefully over the sound of the rushing water and you might hear ruby-crowned kinglets, Swainson's thrushes, and parula warblers. On your drive in, stop to listen and look for mourning warblers.

Directions: *From the junction of Routes 3 and 145 in Pittsburg, go south on Rte. 3 for 2.5 miles to Jesse Young Road, a town road. Turn north and drive to the 1-mile marker, where the road becomes a one-lane, seasonal, privately maintained gravel logging road. Pass at your own risk. LOGGING TRUCKS HAVE THE RIGHT OF WAY FROM THIS POINT ON. Continue northward with care. You will pass through an orange gate near the 5-mile marker. Above the 12-mile marker, you will see Depot Camp, a large clearing with two cabins. Go straight. Continue to a fork above the 13-mile marker. The left road leads to Perley Terrill Dam, so go straight. Continue to the canyon parking area above the 16-mile marker. You are now about 16.5 miles from Rte. 3. Safe driving time is about 40 minutes one-way. The road is closed in the winter and during mud season. Weather or road conditions may close the road without notice.*

Ownership: Champion International Corporation (603) 246-3331

Size: 50 acres   **Closest Town:** Pittsburg

New Hampshire has two kinds of weasels.
Long-tailed weasels are found most frequently in the
forests. Ermines inhabit forest edges and openings.
In winter, ermines change to a coat of white,
except for the black tips on their tails.

2. CONNECTICUT LAKES STATE FOREST

Description: Known locally as George D. Roberts Park, the Connecticut Lakes State Forest is a narrow strip of land along Route 3, extending from just above Second Connecticut Lake to the Canadian border. The area is predominantly spruce-fir forest. Parking is available at pull-offs.

Viewing Information: This section of Route 3 is known as "moose alley." If you travel along this road on a summer evening, you are virtually assured of seeing a moose. June is the best time to see and hear the neotropical migrants that nest here, among them Tennessee, black-throated blue, black-throated green, and mourning warblers. Other summer residents include olive-sided, least, and alder flycatchers as well as solitary, Philadelphia, and red-eyed vireos. Resident birds include ruffed grouse, gray jays, black-backed and pileated woodpeckers, purple finches, and boreal chickadees.

Directions: *From Pittsburg, take Route 3 north.*

Ownership: DRED—Division of Forest and Lands (603) 271-3456

Size: 1,548 acres   **Closest Town:** Pittsburg

In winter the large, furred hind feet tracks of the snowshoe hare are easily identified. Snowshoe hares have been clocked at 31 miles an hour.
TOM & PAT LEESON

Description: This typical northwoods pond is surrounded by spruce-fir forest. An area next to the dam allows you to launch a canoe for a better look.

Viewing Information: If you have a canoe, paddle northeast from the dam for approximately 1 mile. Early morning is the best time to find moose feeding on aquatic plants. You should be able to spot an array of boreal forest birds, including boreal chickadees, ruby-crowned kinglets, and magnolia and blackpoll warblers. Other interesting birds often sighted here include spruce grouse, common snipes, common goldeneyes, American black ducks, common ravens, gray jays, and black-backed woodpeckers. Adjacent lands are owned by The Nature Conservancy.

Directions: From the Second Connecticut Lake dam, travel 3.1 miles north on Route 3. Where Rte. 3 curves sharply left, turn right on an unmarked, privately maintained gravel road. LOGGING TRUCKS HAVE THE RIGHT OF WAY FROM THIS POINT ON. After 0.3 mile, the road crosses a wooden bridge and then comes to a T. Turn right at the T and continue for 1 mile. At the fork, go left for another 0.7 mile. Turn left at the dam to the Fish and Game Department boat launch. The road is closed in the winter and during mud season. Weather or road conditions may close the road without notice.

Ownership: Champion International Corporation (603) 246-3331

Size: 83 acres   **Closest Town:** Pittsburg

Birds of the spruce-fir forest, spruce grouse survive on the buds and needles of evergreen trees in the winter. During summer they eat insects, seeds, fruits, tender leaves, and mushrooms. CHARLES H. WILLEY

4. MAGALLOWAY MOUNTAIN

Description: An approximately 1-mile trail through spruce-fir forests leads to the fire lookout tower atop Magalloway Mountain. A forest fire watcher from the Department of Resources and Economic Development—Division of Forests and Lands is present at some times of year and is happy to answer questions. Depending upon visibility, you may be able to see parts of New Hampshire, Vermont, Maine, and Quebec. A large part of what you see is a working forest owned by Champion and other forest resource companies.

Viewing Information: On the hike to the tower, you may see a variety of birds and animals. Look for ravens, broad-winged hawks, and red-tailed hawks. If you don't see a moose you are almost sure to see signs of them. Depending upon the time of day, visitors often see deer, snowshoe hares, and red squirrels.

Directions: *From the junction of Routes 3 and 145 in Pittsburg, travel north on Rte. 3 for about 12 miles to Magalloway Road, a one-lane, seasonal, privately maintained gravel logging road. LOGGING TRUCKS HAVE THE RIGHT OF WAY FROM THIS POINT ON. Go east on Magalloway Road to a bridge and a fork just past the 1-mile marker. Bear to the right. Continue to a fork just past the 2-mile marker; bear left. Go uphill to a fork just short of the 3-mile marker; bear left again. Drive through a large, open gravel pit and past the 5-mile marker to the junction with Fire Tower Road. Make a sharp right turn onto Fire Tower Road. Continue for about 3 miles to the trailhead sign. The trailhead is 8 miles from Rte. 3. Parking is limited. Park parallel to the gravel road, leaving room for other cars to drive by. Safe driving time is 30 minutes one way. The road is closed in winter and during mud season. Weather or road conditions may close the road without notice.*

Ownership: Champion International Corporation (603) 246-3331

Size: 1-mile trail   **Closest Town:** Pittsburg

Before you use your binoculars, find an animal with your eyes by watching for movement. Once you have spotted a bird or mammal, note a point of reference such as a forked limb. Without taking your eyes from the spot, slowly lift the binoculars into position and focus.

Description: A short trail through spruce-fir forest brings you to the overlook of this scenic 40-foot waterfall. Owned by Champion, Garfield Falls is a 98-acre "Special Place in the Forest." *BE CAREFUL—THE TRAIL HAS STEEP DROP-OFFS AND MAY BE SLIPPERY.*

Viewing Information: Keep your eyes open on the drive in; wildlife may be around any curve. As in other parts of the northern forest, you may see moose here during the summer. Look for snowshoe hares and red squirrels; also expect to see ruffed grouse, white-throated sparrows, Cape May warblers, and a variety of other birds.

Directions: *From the junction of Routes 3 and 145 in Pittsburg, travel north on Rte. 3 for about 12 miles to Magalloway Road, a one-lane, seasonal, privately maintained gravel logging road. LOGGING TRUCKS HAVE THE RIGHT OF WAY FROM THIS POINT ON. Go east on Magalloway Road to a bridge and a fork just past the 1-mile marker. Bear to the right. Continue to a fork just past the 2-mile marker; bear left. Go uphill to a fork just short of the 3-mile marker; bear left again. Drive through a large, open gravel pit and on past the 5-mile marker to the junction with Fire Tower Road. Keep going straight, past the 8-mile marker, to a fork; bear left. Go up and over a ridge and past the 9-mile marker to another fork; bear right. Keep bearing right along the road most heavily used, past the 10-mile marker, to an intersection close to a bridge. Go straight. The road is narrow and more difficult to travel on from this point. Continue south about 1.4 miles to the trailhead sign. The trailhead is 12 miles from Rte. 3. Safe driving time is about 30 minutes one way. The road is closed in winter and during mud season. Weather or road conditions may close the road without notice.*

Ownership: Champion International Corporation (603) 246-3331

Size: 98 acres   **Closest Town:** Pittsburg

Little is known about the breeding habits of evening grosbeaks that nest in the coniferous forest of northern New Hampshire. Large flocks of grosbeaks are periodically seen during winter at backyard feeders.
MARK & SUE WERNER

6. THE BALSAMS

Description: The property surrounds a four-star grand resort hotel in scenic Dixville Notch.

Viewing Information: Opportunities for viewing wildlife against the rugged backdrop of Dixville Notch occur throughout the year. Peregrine falcons return to their nesting site on the cliffs of Mount Abeniki in March and are active in the area until late July. Look for moose in Two Town Pond and on the golf course. In the winter, watch for pine marten tracks on the remote cross-country ski trails. Bicknell's thrushes inhabit the spruce-fir forest. The BALSAMS is a good place to see and hear Blackburnian and magnolia warblers as well as a myriad of other migratory songbirds. You may even find boreal chickadees and black-backed three-toed woodpeckers.

Directions: *From the junction of Routes 3 and 26 in Colebrook, travel 10.2 miles east on Rte. 26. People who are not registered at the hotel must pay a trail fee in summer and winter.*

Ownership: Private ownership; leased to the BALSAMS Corporation (603) 255-3400

Size: 15,000 acres   **Closest Town:** Dixville

The cliffs of Mt. Abeniki rising behind the BALSAMS Grand Hotel provide perfect nesting habitat for peregrine falcons. Reaching speeds of up to 200 miles per hour, peregrines snatch other birds in mid-air.
GEORGE WUERTHNER

Description: The viewing area allows visitors to see the abundance and variety of wildlife that use a regenerating northern forest. Forestry management is active here. An accessible interpretive trail and viewing blind were constructed in 1996.

Viewing Information: In the spring and early summer, there are plentiful opportunities to view moose and deer. A large lick—a place where road salt collects in a wet area—provides moose with important minerals. The moose may be there at any time of day, but the best viewing time is in the early morning or evening. Colorful wood warblers, such as mourning, chestnut-sided, and common yellowthroat, nest in the shrubs. Listen for purple finches, white-throated sparrows, and kinglets in the larger spruce and fir trees.

Directions: From the junction of Routes 16 and 26 in Errol, drive west on Rte. 26 for 9.8 miles. The parking lot is on the left.

Ownership: Boise Cascade; viewing area managed by NHFG (603) 271-3211

Size: 5 acres   **Closest Town:** Errol

To meet their dietary needs in winter, moose seek out hardwood and evergreen areas, where they eat only twigs and buds. Their summer diet includes aquatic vegetation.
CHARLES H. WILLEY

Description: This is New Hampshire's premier watchable wildlife site and the 495th designated national wildlife refuge. The wetlands and spruce-fir forest are home to many of the animals people like to watch. The interior of the refuge is accessible only by water. A headquarters building provides information about the refuge. Adjoining properties, including Lake Umbagog State Park, increase the size of the area protected for conservation purposes.

Viewing Information: Wildlife waits around every bend. The Leonard Pond area boasts the only pair of nesting bald eagles in the state. Common loons are abundant, with more than twenty nesting pairs on the lake. More than ten pairs of ospreys nest in the surrounding area. Visitors often see moose snacking on the aquatic vegetation. Frequent sightings of eastern kingbirds, belted kingfishers, and great blue herons are reported. Early summer is a great time to listen for woodland songbirds such as winter wrens, golden-crowned kinglets, northern parula warblers, black-throated blue warblers, and white-throated sparrows. During fall migration, shorebirds and waterfowl use the area for resting and feeding.

Directions: *The refuge headquarters is located on Route 16, 5.5 miles north of Errol. There are boat access sites off Rte. 26 and Rte. 16.*

Ownership: USFWS (603) 482-3415

Size: 4,106 acres   **Closest Town:** Errol

NORTHERN

Moose are New Hampshire's largest mammals, sometimes weighing over 1,100 pounds. They live primarily in ever-green forests but are found throughout the state. In summer, moose eat aquatic vegetation and browse on leaves and twigs. Their winter diet is restricted to bark, twigs, and buds. Look for moose in "licks" along the roadside, where salt from the highway has collected in culvert areas.

Description: This is not only one of New Hampshire's most scenic roads, it is also known as "the" place to find a variety of northwoods wildlife.

Viewing Information: The 13-mile stretch of road winds along the Androscoggin River. Scenic easements from adjacent landowners allow for public use of this area of spruce-fir forest and rushing river. Interpretive signs are provided at Bog Brook, Androscoggin Wayside, and Mollidgewock Campground. Be alert for moose along the roadway from April through September. In late spring and early summer, you can generally see moose at any time of day; in the early morning and late evening hours, a sighting is almost a certainty. Look overhead for ospreys; watch the river for common loons and mergansers. Evening grosbeaks, boreal chickadees, and northern three-toed woodpeckers are found here. Cape May, blackpoll, and yellow-throated warblers make their summer homes in the area. Great blue herons often fish in the slower portions of the river. Canoeing and fishing are common recreational activities on this stretch of the river.

Directions: *The 13 miles stretch from Errol south on Route 16 to 1.5 miles past the Dummer-Cambridge town line.*

Ownership: Crown Vantage-Wagner Woodlands (scenic easement held by State of New Hampshire DOT; campground managed by DRED—Division of Parks and Recreation (603) 271-3556)

Size: 13-mile drive   **Closest Town:** Errol

An osprey, also known as a fish hawk, hovers over the water until a fish nears the surface, then it dives feet first to seize the prey in its talons. Until the early 1990s, the ospreys nested only in northern New Hampshire; now they also nest on Great Bay. CHARLES H. WILLEY

10. PONTOOK RESERVOIR

Description: The Pontook Dam on the Androscoggin River forms this reservoir and wetland area. Spruce-fir forest surrounds the dam site, which has a recreation area with interpretive signs, viewing area, and boat launch. Pontook Reservoir is a wonderful place to look for wildlife; the many pull-offs along Route 16 allow for good viewing even without a canoe.

Viewing Information: In the spring and summer, early morning and late evening are excellent times to look for moose. The wetlands provide a nesting area for a variety of birds, including American bitterns, pied-billed grebes, common loons, wood ducks, hooded mergansers, and American black and ring-necked ducks. Ospreys and kingfishers are frequently seen fishing over the water. Great blue herons wade in the shallows. Watch for northern harriers flying over the marsh. Common yellowthroats, olive-sided, and alder flycatchers, Nashville warblers, northern waterthrushes, and bay-breasted warblers are all possibilities.

Directions: From Milan, travel north on Route 16 for approximately 8 miles.

Ownership: Pontook Limited Partnership, Water Resources

Size: 300 acres   **Closest Town:** Milan

11. WEEKS STATE PARK

Description: The park is the former summer estate of John Wingate Weeks. As a U.S. senator, he established the Weeks Act, which created the National Forest system. The narrow 1.5-mile road to the summit of Mount Prospect is a New Hampshire Scenic Byway; it is not wide enough for buses or campers. When the entrance gate is closed, visitors can access the park and summit on foot. A house with exhibits, a fire-lookout tower, and gardens await those who venture to the top. The road and trails travel through a diverse woodland of spruce, white pine, paper birch, and sugar maple.

Viewing Information: During the fall hawk migration, the summit is a good place to view broad-winged and sharp-shinned hawks, bald eagles, peregrine falcons, and ospreys as they head south. Moose and deer inhabit the area, as well as other mammals found in the North Country. A wide array of songbirds nests in the park.

Directions: From the junction of Routes 2 and 3 in Lancaster, drive 2.4 miles south on Rte. 3 to the park entrance on the left.

Ownership: DRED—Division of Parks and Recreation (603) 271-3556

Size: 446 acres   **Closest Town:** Lancaster

Description: Nestled in the White Mountains north of the Presidential Range, the Pondicherry Wildlife Refuge was designated a National Natural Landmark in 1974. The refuge consists of Big and Little Cherry ponds. No roads lead to the ponds; however, you can reach Big Cherry pond from near the Whitefield airport by a trail following the old Maine Central Railroad snowmobile corridor. Big and Little Cherry Ponds are completely natural, having been created by beaver dams. Both are somewhat marshy and contain much submerged, floating, and emergent vegetation. Of significance are the sixty acres of nearly open sphagnum and heath bog mat which surround Big Cherry Pond and a black spruce-tamarack bog forest.

Viewing Information: Moose and white-tailed deer frequent the area, and there is considerable beaver activity. The two ponds are important breeding areas for green-winged teal, ring-necked ducks, American black ducks, wood ducks, and, occasionally, hooded mergansers. Other birds known to spend the summer at the ponds include pied-billed grebes, great blue herons, American bitterns, northern harriers, Virginia and sora rails, common snipes, mourning and Wilson's warblers, rusty blackbirds, and Lincoln's sparrows. More than forty species of water birds have been recorded during migration periods.

Directions: *From Route 3 in Whitefield, follow signs for Whitefield Airport. Continue on Hazen Road until you are across from the power plant. You will find a parking area and an access trail along the old Maine Central Railroad snowmobile corridor.*

Ownership: ASNH (603 224-9909); management agreement with NHFG

Size: 310 acres   **Closest Towns:** Whitefield and Jefferson

Once extirpated from New Hampshire and the eastern United States due to pesticide contamination, loss of habitat, and human disturbance, the peregrine falcon is making a comeback today. During the mid-1970s, captive-reared peregrines were reintroduced on cliffs where they traditionally nested. Today, these birds and their offspring are returning to nest sites in Franconia Notch, Crawford Notch, Mt. Abeniki, Cathedral Ledge, Devils Slide, and Holts Ledge.

Shy and well camouflaged, American bitterns are seldom seen. They are known to abandon a marsh at the slightest disturbance. Listen for their unusual call, somtimes described as sounding like rusty plumbing—"oong-KA-chunk."
CHARLES H. WILLEY

13. THE ROCKS ESTATE

Description: The estate is a fine example of a 19th-century gentleman's residence, complete with sugarbush, managed forest, a Christmas tree plantation, and open fields. Architecture buffs will enjoy viewing the buildings and gardens. The estate offers educational activities and interpretive trails. Boulder-studded fields provide superb views of the Presidential Range of the White Mountains.

Viewing Information: Diversity in the landscape results in the variety of wildlife found here. Visitors can see or find evidence of a number of mammals, including deer, moose, foxes, red squirrels, wild turkeys, and bears. In the spring and summer, look for bobolinks and other field-loving songbirds. Cedar waxwings, purple finches, hairy and downy woodpeckers, and a variety of warblers are commonly sighted.

Directions: *Follow Interstate 93 to exit 40. Go east 0.1 mile on Route 302 and park at the Red Barns Wayside Area on the right. If you are attending a scheduled program, proceed another 0.2 mile to the main entrance and park in the designated parking lot behind the large barn.*

Ownership: SPNHF (603) 444-6228

Size: 1,371 acres   **Closest Town:** Bethlehem

New Hampshire has a healthy black bear population, which has been expanding its range during the past ten years. Black bears hibernate for six to seven months a year. During that time they do not eat, urinate, or defecate. JOHN H. GAVIN

14. ZEALAND VALLEY

Description: The Zeeland Valley Road provides access to a portion of the White Mountain National Forest. A number of trails leave from parking areas along the road. Hikers will find great diversity on trails that lead first through paper birch, maple, and beech forest, then through balsam fir and red spruce forest. The road follows the Zeeland River, traveling through riparian habitat.

Viewing Information: It is possible to see wildlife from a car, but your chances increase if you decide to take a hike. Be prepared with a detailed map, proper clothing and footwear, and water. In summer, moose are common in the valley, as are a variety of birds including common yellowthroats, black-throated green warblers, and black-throated blue warblers. As you move to higher elevations, look for white-throated sparrows, dark-eyed juncos, and gray jays. If you are lucky, you may see a spruce grouse.

Directions: From the junction of Routes 3 and 302 in Twin Mountain, travel east on Rte. 302 for 2.2 miles. Turn right on Zeeland Road.

Ownership: USFS (603) 869-2626 or TTY (603) 867-3104

Size: 763,502 acres   **Closest Town:** Twin Mountain

15. CRAWFORD NOTCH STATE PARK

Description: Crawford Notch was shaped by the last continental glacier. It is a place of rugged beauty and tumbling water. Trails leaving from just outside the state park access the summits of the White Mountains' Presidential Range. A visitors' facility located near the former site of the Willey House has a pictur-esque small pond and a short walking trail.

Viewing Information: Like Franconia Notch, Crawford Notch is the summer home of a pair of peregrine falcons. Locating the birds on the large cliffs requires binoculars or a spotting scope. Watch for moose along the stream areas in the summer. If you look closely in areas where American beeches grow, you will find evidence of black bears. Watch and listen for red-breasted nuthatches, golden-crowned kinglets, yellow-rumped and blackpoll warblers, white-throated spar-rows, and dark-eyed juncos. Common ravens soar overhead. To see or hear birds of the boreal forest, such as boreal chickadees, winter wrens, Swainson's thrushes, or Blackburnian warblers, take the rugged Webster-Jackson trail to the summit of Mount Jackson. (This is actually on USFS land.) You may be rewarded with a rare sighting of a three-toed woodpecker.

Directions: The park is located along Route 302 between Bretton Woods and Bartlett.

Ownership: DRED—Division of Parks and Recreation (603) 271-3556

Size: 5,950 acres   **Closest Town:** Bartlett

NORTHERN

16. LOST POND

Description: A 0.5-mile walk along the Ellis River through northern hardwoods and balsam fir brings you to Lost Pond.

Viewing Information: Walkers often see moose in and around an old beaver pond that sits at the beginning of the trail to Lost Pond. On the trail, listen for a variety of neotropical birds, including black-throated blue, black-throated green, and black-and-white warblers. You may also detect the songs of Canada and Blackburnian warblers. Hearing the "Old Sam Peabody, Peabody, Peabody" call of the white-throated sparrow is almost a sure bet. Watch for evidence of beavers and otters along the banks of the river.

Directions: *The pond is on Route 16 in Pinkham Notch. Park at the Appalachian Mountain Club parking area, which is north of Jackson and south of Gorham. The Lost Pond trail begins across the road from the AMC parking area.*

Ownership: USFS (603) 466-2713 or TYY (603) 466-2856

Size: 0.5-mile trail **Closest Town:** Gorham

17. BASIN POND

Description: Cliffs surround manmade Basin Pond on three sides. The area immediately around the pond is a combination of fields, marshes, and mixed woodland of maple, beech, birch, spruce, and balsam fir. Non-motorized boat access is available.

Viewing Information: Moose and beaver are common here. Look for songbirds such as Canada warblers, American redstarts, black-throated blue warblers, and black-throated green warblers in the late spring and summer. In the fall, you will likely see a variety of waterfowl including ring-necked ducks, American black ducks, mergansers, and green-winged teal.

Directions: *From Center Conway, travel north on Route 113 to North Chatham. This stretch of Rte. 113 crosses back and forth between Maine and New Hampshire several times. Approximately 1.8 miles north of North Chatham, turn left at the U.S. Forest Service sign for Basin Pond Campground.*

Ownership: USFS (603) 447-5448 or TTY (603) 447-1989

Size: 23-acre pond **Closest Town:** Fryeburg, Maine

18. MOUNTAIN POND

Description: A 2.6-mile trail circles the pond, passing through a diverse mix of habitats for over eighty species of nesting birds.

Viewing Information: Near the start of the trail, look along the swamp edges for rusty blackbirds, spotted sandpipers, belted kingfishers, ruby-throated hummingbirds, tree swallows, Nashville warblers, common yellowthroats, and swamp sparrows. The trail intersects the outlet of Mountain Pond, which may be difficult to cross at high water. Be alert here for yellow-bellied sapsuckers, veeries, hermit thrushes, and black-throated blue, magnolia, and yellow-rumped warblers. A pair of common loons lives at the pond in the summer. Look for green and great blue herons, wood ducks, and American black ducks too. If you are lucky, you might see beavers. Just north of Mountain Pond is a designated Natural Research Area of uncut hardwoods. Huge sugar maples, white ashes, yellow birches, and basswoods, some over 200 years old, have survived in this 132-acre patch. The woods harbor purple finches, hairy woodpeckers, black-throated green and black-and-white warblers, and ruffed grouse.

Directions: From North Conway, travel north on Route 16. In Bartlett, turn right on Town Hall Road. When you reach the intersection with Rte. 16A, continue straight onto Slippery Brook Road. After 2.4 miles, the pavement ends and a small road enters from the right; continue straight here. You will see a White Mountain National Forest sign 0.8 mile later. Just beyond the sign, the road passes through a gate. (From here the road is not plowed in winter.) Proceed 2.6 miles, stay right at the fork, and go another 0.6 mile to the sign for Mountain Pond Trail. Park on the right.

Ownership: White Mountain National Forest (603) 447-5448 or TTY (603) 447-1989

Size: 80-acre pond   **Closest Town:** North Conway

Gleaning insects from twigs and leaves, the colorful magnolia warbler is often associated with woodland edges and clearings. Listen for its "weeta, weeta, weetsee," with the last note rising.
JOHN H. GAVIN

41

Description: Perhaps best known as the home of the state's symbol, the Old Man of the Mountain rock formation, Franconia Notch State Park has many geologic features including the Flume, the Basin, and Cannon Cliffs. A variety of wildlife can be seen throughout the park. A full complement of park facilities is available. Numerous trails lead to the higher summits of Mounts Lafayette, Lincoln, and Liberty, and an aerial tramway can take you to the top of Cannon Mountain.

Viewing Information: As early as mid-March, scan Cannon and Eagle cliffs for a view of peregrine falcons. A pair has nested here since the early 1980s. Early June mornings are the time to look for black bears on the slopes of the Cannon Ski Area. Visitors often see moose at Echo Lake in the spring and summer. A variety of resident and migratory birds nests in the park. Use the aerial tramway to access the summit of 4,180-foot Cannon Mountain. Listen for Bicknell's thrushes at the top, and look for gray jays, boreal chickadees, and white-throated sparrows.

Directions: *A section of Interstate 93 just north of exit 33 is designated as the Franconia Notch Parkway. The parkway provides limited access to the Flume, the Basin, Lafayette Campground, trailhead parking spots, Boise Rock, the Profile, Cannon Ski Area, and Echo Lake.*

Ownership: DRED—Division of Parks and Recreation (603)271-3556

Size: 6,693 acres   **Closest Town:** Franconia

In late March, look for peregrine falcons against the magnificent backdrop of the Cannon Cliffs in Franconia Notch State Park. GEORGE WUERTHNER

42

20. KANCAMAGUS SCENIC BYWAY

Description: The 34.5-mile route between Lincoln and Conway provides stunning views of White Mountain National Forest, one of the most visited national forests in the country. The byway rises to nearly 3,000 feet as it crosses the north side of Mount Kancamagus and then slowly descends. The road passes through northern hardwood and spruce-fir forest. You will find several campgrounds, picnic sites, trailheads, and scenic overlooks along the highway.

Viewing Information: The scenic byway offers several opportunities to stop and take short walks; this is the best way to experience and learn about the wildlife found in the area. You are likely to see moose during the spring and summer, especially in the early morning and evening hours, and especially in the vicinity of Oliverian Brook. WATCH FOR MOOSE CROSSING THE ROAD. In the summer, a wide array of neotropical migrants nests in the forest. Birds found here year-round include ravens, black-capped and boreal chickadees, purple finches, gray jays, dark-eyed juncos, and nuthatches.

Directions: Take Route 112 between Lincoln and Conway.

Ownership: USFS (603) 447-5448/(603) 536-1310 or TTY (603) 447-1989

Size: 34.5-mile drive   **Closest Towns:** Lincoln, Conway

21. LIVERMORE FALLS

Description: A scenic area along the Pemigewasset River, Livermore Falls was the site of the state's first fish hatchery. Atlantic salmon traditionally used the pool at the base of the falls in the summer; here they gathered, waiting for the right time to continue their upstream journey to spawn. The area features a forested bluff and a small floodplain.

Viewing Information: A short trail provides access to the floodplain and river. In early May, migratory songbirds use the river corridor as they make their way north. Common yellowthroats and song sparrows nest along the river. Look for evidence of raccoons, otters, and minks.

Directions: Take exit 25 off Interstate 93. Turn left, drive 0.2 mile, and then turn left onto Route 175. Proceed 1.5 miles to Livermore Falls Road and turn left. The parking lot is less than 0.1 mile farther, on the left. A trail leads down to the river.

Ownership: DRED; cooperative management agreement with NHFG (603) 271-3211

Size: 44 acres   **Closest Town:** Plymouth

REGION 2—NEW HAMPSHIRE UPLANDS

The southwestern portion of the state is a sloping plateau with many small lakes and narrow valley streams. The landscape is dotted with isolated hills and peaks of hard, resistant rock called monadnocks. The Connecticut River valley, like the Merrimack River valley to the east, is filled with glacial outwash and glacial lake deposits.

As you travel from south to north, the forest changes from oak, white pine, and hemlock to sugar maple, American Beech, red spruce, and balsam fir. Prior to the Civil War, most of this area was taken up with agricultural production. Today, farms are active in the Connecticut River valley, but much of the other land in the area has reverted to woodlands.

The landscape provides habitat for wild turkeys, pileated woodpeckers, wood thrushes, white-tailed deer, moose, and bears. In the spring, vernal pools become a haven for spring peepers, wood frogs, and yellow-spotted salamanders. The Connecticut River supports the endangered dwarf wedge mussel and the tiger cobblestone beetle.

Picturesque streams surrounded by forests are part of the landscape of western New Hampshire. Autumn scenes become brilliant as maple, beech, and birch trees change to crimson, yellow, and gold. CHARLES H. WILLEY

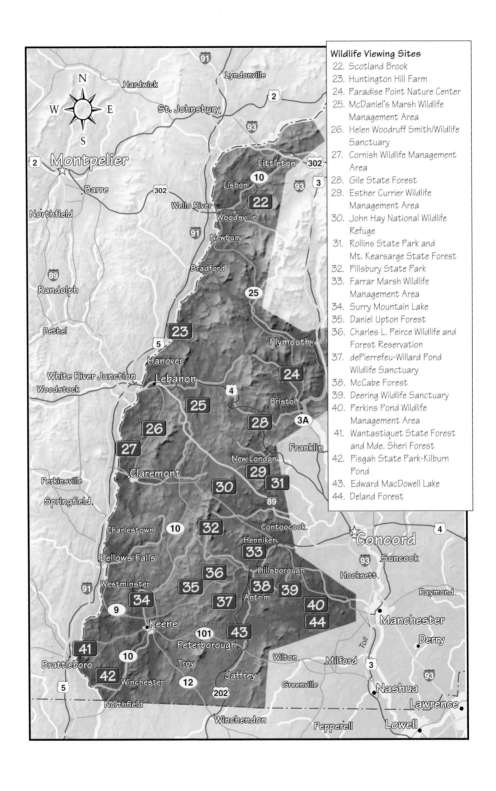

Wildlife Viewing Sites
22. Scotland Brook
23. Huntington Hill Farm
24. Paradise Point Nature Center
25. McDaniel's Marsh Wildlife Management Area
26. Helen Woodruff Smith/Wildlife Sanctuary
27. Cornish Wildlife Management Area
28. Gile State Forest
29. Esther Currier Wildlife Management Area
30. John Hay National Wildlife Refuge
31. Rollins State Park and Mt. Kearsarge State Forest
32. Pillsbury State Park
33. Farrar Marsh Wildlife Management Area
34. Surry Mountain Lake
35. Daniel Upton Forest
36. Charles L. Peirce Wildlife and Forest Reservation
37. dePierrefeu-Willard Pond Wildlife Sanctuary
38. McCabe Forest
39. Deering Wildlife Sanctuary
40. Perkins Pond Wildlife Management Area
41. Wantastiquet State Forest and Mde. Sheri Forest
42. Pisgah State Park-Kilburn Pond
43. Edward MacDowell Lake
44. Deland Forest

RED-TAILED HAWK

WHITE PINE

WHITE-TAILED DEER

TIGER SWALLOWTAIL

EASTERN HEMLOCK

WOOD DUCK

PINK LADY'S SLIPPER

SPRING PEEPER

PUMPKIN SEED

Southern New Hampshire

The fields and forests of southern New Hampshire are complex communities of plants and animals that change constantly as they grow and interact. The oaks and white pines make way for maple and beech forests but persist in the woodlands of the Connecticut and Merrimack valleys far into the northern

ROSE-BREASTED GROSBEAK

GRAY SQUIRREL

RED FOX

RED OAK

WILD TURKEY

EASTERN PAINTED TURTLE

ARROWHEAD

YELLOW PERCH

BLACK-WINGED DAMSELFLY

hardwood region. A foray into the woods during any season will reward you with a glimpse or sign of the varied wildlife. During spring and summer listen for the songs of rose-breasted grosbeaks, hermit thrushes, and American redstarts. Tracks in the winter snow tell us white-tailed deer, wild turkeys, and gray squirrels live here year-round.

Description: A brook, fields, wetlands, northern hardwood forest, and spruce-fir forest are here to explore. The area supports a large variety of fauna including twenty-two kinds of mammals, eighty-six bird species, four species of reptiles, and eleven kinds of amphibians. One area is managed for field-grown balsams. Trails provide access to the diverse habitats.

Viewing Information: Moose, black bears, white-tailed deer, porcupines, and fishers live here. Snowshoe hares use the low conifers for cover and winter forage. In the spring, the woods are filled with song. Listen for hermit and wood thrushes, black-and-white warblers, Blackburnian warblers, red-eyed vireos, and rose-breasted grosbeaks. The diverse bird life during the summer includes chestnut-sided warblers, white-throated sparrows, chipping sparrows, magnolia warblers, and ovenbirds. Beavers move in and out of the area, creating wetlands. You may see water-loving birds such as belted kingfishers, great blue herons, wood ducks, and American black ducks feeding in the wetlands. The wetlands also provide nesting habitat for olive-sided and alder flycatchers and northern parula warblers.

Directions: *Take exit 38 off Interstate 93 in Franconia. Turn left at the bottom of the ramp, then go right onto Routes 116 /18 north. When you get to Rte. 117, turn left. Go 3 miles to Sugar Hill and turn left onto Pearl Lake Road. After 3.5 miles, just past Pearl Lake, Pearl Lake Road turns left. Keep going for 2.2 miles, then turn left onto Jim Noyes Hill Road. Look for the trailhead sign across from Scotland School (private property).*

Ownership: ASNH (603) 224-9909

Size: 102 acres   **Closest Town:** Franconia

New Hampshire has a healthy population of between 2,500 and 3,000 black bears. Most active from May through October, they feed heavily on greens, nuts, berries, carrion, insects, and small mammals. In late fall, they enter their dens and fall into a deep winter sleep. NEVER approach or feed a bear.

23. HUNTINGTON HILL FARM

Description: The first Wildlife Stewardship Award presented in the state went to Huntington Hill Farm. The farm's land is protected by a conservation easement, and the farm provides demonstration areas for different types of habitat management including forest, field, wetland, and riparian.

Viewing Information: The farm has more than 3.5 miles of walking trails. *FOOT TRAVEL ONLY PLEASE.* Depending upon the time of year, you can see—or see signs of—many species of wildlife. Watch for deer and moose, especially in the late evening or early morning. A variety of neotropical migrants arrives in the summer, including bobolinks, chestnut-sided warblers, indigo buntings, redstarts, red-eyed vireos, and scarlet tanagers. Tree swallows and bluebirds take advantage of the nest boxes provided around the open fields. The aspen stands are home to ruffed grouse.

Directions: *From the center of Etna, go 3.6 miles north on the main road (Two-Mile Road) to Goodfellow Road. Turn left on Goodfellow Road and drive 0.6 mile. A number of access sites marked "Foot Travel Only" lead to trails; there is also access to the parking provided at Huntington Hill Farm.*

Ownership: Sam Doyle, Conservation Easement (603) 643-2801

Size: 439 acres   **Closest Town:** Hanover Center

Catching a glimpse of a New Hampshire's state mammal is always a thrill. White-tailed deer are animals of the forest edge. In severe winter weather, they "yard up" in dense stands of mature evergreen trees. CHARLES H. WILLEY

Description: Located on the north shore of Newfound Lake, Paradise Point Nature Center offers an array of programs during the summer months. The unspoiled lakeshore is bounded by a mature forest of hemlock, red spruce, and white pine. Hebron Marsh, just a short distance from here, has a wildlife viewing platform. The center is universally accessible. Trails are open year-round from dawn to dusk; ask at the center for a trail guide.

Viewing Information: Trails provide access to the lake and allow you to explore this beautiful area. On the trail, keep your senses alert for signs of wildlife: the drilling of pileated woodpeckers, the song of the winter wren, the tracks of a red fox. Snags provide dens and nesting sites for chickadees, flying squirrels, and downy and hairy woodpeckers. Spring and early summer are good times to look in vernal pools for eggs, tadpoles, or adult amphibians such as spring peepers and red-spotted newts. In the summer, listen for the call of common loons, watch for mergansers, and find evidence of minks on the trail along the lake.

Directions: *From Bristol, go north on Route 3A for 9 miles (you will pass through East Hebron). Turn left onto North Shore Road and drive 1 mile. The sign for the nature center's driveway is on the left. From Plymouth, take Rte. 25 west to Rte. 3A south. Follow Rte. 3A south for 5 miles and turn right onto North Shore Road. Hebron Marsh is another 1.2 miles down the road.*

Ownership: ASNH (603) 224-9909. Call for summer programs list.

Size: 43 acres   **Closest Town:** Plymouth

Vernal pools are temporary water sources. Fed by snowmelt and rain, they lose most of their water by late summer. In spring and into summer, vernal pools teem with frogs, salamanders, newts, fairy shrimp, and insects. Wood frogs, spring peepers, and spotted salamanders breed in vernal pools, depending on the pools for species survival.

Description: Mixed hardwood and softwood forest surrounds the 300-acre open marsh. The marsh is an excellent place to examine emergent, floating, and submerged plants.

Viewing Information: Bring your canoe to get the best look at this site. Wildlife is abundant; visitors can see everything from moose to minks. Wood duck nest boxes throughout the marsh area provide nesting sites for hooded and common mergansers as well as wood ducks. Look for belted kingfishers, yellow-rumped warblers, common yellowthroats, and song sparrows. In past years, the state-endangered pied-billed grebe has nested here. Do not approach a grebe between April and August; they are very susceptible to human disturbance. The area is managed for waterfowl production and is used as a stopover for migrants in the fall. The upland habitat provides cover for ruffed grouse, white-tailed deer, and snowshoe hares.

Directions: *From Enfield Center on Route 4A, turn south onto Bog Road at George Pond. Follow Bog Road for about 4.4 miles to its junction with George Hill Road at Washburn corner. Dam, marsh, parking lot, and launching ramp will be on your left.*

Ownership: NHFG (603) 271-3211

Size: 513 acres   **Closest Town:** Enfield Center

Slipping quietly through wildlife habitat in a canoe is often a great way to catch a glimpse of wary species. Paddle slowly or simply float silently scanning the streamside vegetation and the water's edge. CHARLES H. WILLEY

UPLANDS

Description: Located on thirty acres of mature sugar maple and white pine forest in the town of Meriden, the Helen Woodruff Smith Wildlife Sanctuary was among the first of its kind established in the United States.

Viewing Information: A series of walking paths allows for a leisurely tour of the sanctuary. At the entrance, a purple martin house and feeders let you know you have found the right place. Watch for evidence of downy, hairy, and pileated woodpeckers. Scarlet tanagers, red-eyed vireos, and ovenbirds sing frequently in the early summer. Resident birds include black-capped chickadees, white-breasted nuthatches, and brown creepers. The numerous cavities in the old sugar maples make flying squirrel sightings a real possibility. Several plaques and monuments honor those who created and were actively involved in the sanctuary.

Directions: *From Route 120 in the center of Meriden, turn right on Main Street. Go 0.4 mile, passing Kimball Union Academy. As you are descending the hill, look for the entrance to the sanctuary on the right. Parking is available at the Meriden Town Hall.*

Ownership: Meriden Bird Club (603) 469-3493

Size: 30 acres   **Closest Town:** Meriden

Look for oblong or oval holes on large trees as evidence of the presence of pileated woodpeckers. These birds excavate holes that will eventually become homes for barred owls, squirrels, wood ducks, and other forest animals.
CHARLES H. WILLEY

27. CORNISH WILDLIFE MANAGEMENT AREA

Description: Located in the cornfields along the Connecticut River, the management area is a riparian habitat. Visitors may use the boat launch area (small boats only).

Viewing Information: Bring your canoe down to the river here and take a trip downstream to other access sites. *USE EXTREME CAUTION DURING TIMES OF HIGH WATER.* The riparian corridor along the river provides a variety of summer homes for, among others, belted kingfishers, tree swallows, bank swallows, song sparrows, gray catbirds, common yellowthroats, and red-eyed vireos. During spring and fall migration, the river serves as a natural travelway. Watch for warblers in early May; they spend their summers farther north. A variety of waterfowl stops here in the fall on their way to wintering areas. Beavers, otters, and minks live on the river's edge; the banks also provide important habitat components for deer, foxes, and coyotes.

Directions: *The management area is on Route 12A, approximately 1 mile north of the Cornish-Winsor covered bridge.*

Ownership: NHFG (603) 271-3211

Size: 29 acres   **Closest Town:** Claremont

28. GILE STATE FOREST—GARDNER MEMORIAL WAYSIDE

Description: This large state forest is made up of northern hardwoods: sugar maple, yellow birch, beech, and balsam fir. Streams, wetlands, and ponds dot the forest.

Viewing Information: An easy half-mile trail leads from the wayside area to scenic Butterfield Pond. Watch for moose tracks and scat near the pond. Coyotes, bears, snowshoe hares, and a variety of other animals live here. Look for wood ducks and hooded mergansers on the pond. In the late spring and summer, the sounds of songbirds fill the woods; listen for ovenbirds, wood thrushes, yellow-throated and red-eyed vireos, rose-breasted grosbeaks, black-throated blue and black-throated green warblers, and scarlet tanagers.

Directions: *The wayside is on Route 4A, 6.8 miles west of the junction of Rtes. 4A and 11.*

Ownership: DRED—Division of Forests and Lands (603) 271-3456

Size: 6,675 acres   **Closest Town:** Springfield

Description: This diverse area is home to a beaver pond, a red maple swamp, a quaking bog, and a mixture of forest types. Visitors can see a fine example of an esker: a gravel ridge created by 10,000-year-old glacial deposits. The site also affords panoramic views of Mount Kearsarge.

Viewing Information: Walk the interpretive trail to get an overview of the area; you will learn about its highly diverse habitats and the wildlife they support. On a quiet walk along the trails, particularly at dawn and dusk, you may spot beavers, otters, porcupines, squirrels, deer, and moose. Other more elusive species include minks, fishers, weasels, foxes, coyotes, and bobcats. In the spring, turtles, frogs, and salamanders are numerous and easy to find. Bird species include both seasonal and year-round residents. Wood ducks, American black ducks, hooded mergansers, and Canada geese all rest here. Visit on an evening in late April or early May and you may get to witness the courtship flights of the American woodcock. In late spring and summer, listen for veeries, wood thrushes, and hermit thrushes during the morning and evening hours. Common yellowthroats, chestnut-sided warblers, and yellow warblers nest in the area for the summer.

Directions: *From exit 11 on Interstate 89, follow Route 11 east for 2.7 miles.*

Ownership: NHFG, New London Conservation Commission (603) 271-3211

Size: 98 acres   **Closest Town:** New London

Active all year, porcupines are mostly creatures of the night. They spend the day perched high in a tree or hidden in a den. As herbivores, they eat twigs, buds, and bark. Porcupines have poor eyesight and rely greatly on hearing and smell.
GEORGE WUERTHNER

30. JOHN HAY NATIONAL WILDLIFE REFUGE, HAY FORESTRY AND WILDLIFE MANAGEMENT AREA, THE FELLS HISTORIC SITE

Description: This unique 1,000-acre area on the shore of Lake Sunapee is cooperatively managed by state and federal agencies, and a nonprofit organization. In the 1800s, then U.S. Secretary of State John Hay acquired the property to establish a summer residence and a large working farm. His son, Clarence Hay, donated parts of the property to the Society for the Protection of New Hampshire Forests and to the U.S. Fish and Wildlife Service. The family home, referred to as "The Fells," is operated as a state historic site, offering interpretive programs. Trails provide access to the woodlands and to Sunset Hill.

Viewing Information: Different seasons bring evidence of a variety of mammals. White-tailed deer, red foxes, and black bears are common in the spring, summer, and fall. Visitors occasionally spot moose in winter. Spring is a good time to look for ruffed grouse and American woodcocks. Keep an eye out for wild turkeys. In the fall, watch for raptors—including broad-winged and sharp-shinned hawks—from Sunset Hill.

Directions: *There are several access points for the area. The entrance to The Fells is on Route 103A north of Newbury. Access to the SPNHF property is also from Rte. 103A. From Rte. 103 in Newbury, go 1.3 miles north on Rte. 103A. Turn right on Rollins Road, go 0.3 mile, and park on the left at the gated south end of Old County Road (don't block the gate). Or continue north on Rte. 103A for another 1.3 miles to Chalk Pond Road. Park here, at the north end of Old County Road, and walk south.*

Ownership: SPNHF (603) 224-9945; USFWS (603) 763-5958; DRED—Division of Parks and Recreation (603) 271-3556

Size: SPNHF: 675 acres; USFWS: 300 acres   **Closest Town:** Newbury

UPLANDS

Because animals are secretive, many wildlife-watching experiences begin with what has been left behind. Look for clues to animals' habits and daily routines. Tracks, droppings, and chewings are the most obvious, but be on the lookout for trails, flattened grass, and holes or nests.

31. ROLLINS STATE PARK AND MOUNT KEARSARGE STATE FOREST

Description: The views from Mount Kearsarge are tremendous. From the summit, you can see ski areas in Vermont, the peaks of the White Mountains, and the closer features of Lake Sunapee, Mount Sunapee, and Ragged Mountain. A road comes within a half mile of the summit on the Warner side.

Viewing Information: The best time of year to visit Mount Kearsarge is in the fall, during hawk migration. Thousands of hawks fly through between mid-September and October. On a clear day in September after a cold front has passed through, you can see hundreds of broad-winged hawks. Sharp-shinned hawks, ospreys, bald eagles, and other raptor species pass over this small mountain as they make their way south. In the summer, look for kestrels, ravens, black-capped chickadees, and Tennessee, black-throated blue, and black-throated green warblers.

Directions: *Take exit 8 off Interstate 89 and turn left at the end of the ramp. At the yield sign, go straight onto Route 103 and continue 1 mile to the center of town. Just beyond the brick town hall, turn right onto Kearsarge Mountain Road. Follow signs to the state park. The Rollins State Park toll booth is 5 miles from the center of town; another 3.5 miles brings you to the end of the road near the summit in Kearsarge State Forest.*

Ownership: DRED—Division of Parks and Recreation (603) 271-3556, DRED—Division of Forests and Lands (603) 271-3456

Size: Rollins State Park: 118 acres; Kearsarge State Forest: 4,965 acres
Closest Town: Warner

The major food sources of red-tailed hawks are small mammals such as mice, chipmunks, and squirrels. When one of these large hawks veers in its soaring, the red on the upper side of its tail can be seen.
JOHN H. GAVIN

32. PILLSBURY STATE PARK

Description: Few visitors disturb this area of ponds, lakes, and wetlands surrounded by forest. Several of the park's trails connect to the Monadnock-Sunapee Greenway. During the summer, the park presents conservation education programs.

Viewing Information: The best way to explore the ponds and lakes is in a canoe. Evidence of beaver work is easy to find; look for the flowages they've created. Park visitors often see otters, muskrats, and minks. The park provides perfect habitat for moose. Turtles, frogs, and small mammals (squirrels and chipmunks) make their homes in the area. Spring heralds the arrival of a variety of wetland and forest songbirds. In the summer, look for wood ducks, hooded mergansers, Canada geese, and loons. During fall migration, diverse waterfowl stop to rest and feed. Watch for raptors such as ospreys, broad-winged hawks, and sharp-shinned hawks flying over Sunapee Ridge.

Directions: Take Route 10 south from Newport through the village of Goshen. Bear left onto Rte. 31. Drive another 4.7 miles to the entrance of the park.

Ownership: DRED—Division of Parks and Recreation (603) 271-3556; DRED—Division of Forests and Lands (603) 271-3456

Size: 8,136 acres   **Closest Town:** Washington

33. FARRAR MARSH WILDLIFE MANAGEMENT AREA

Description: Farrar Marsh offers areas of open water, fields, and a mixed forest of oak and pine.

Viewing Information: An active colony of great blue herons nests here during the spring and summer. *PLEASE DO NOT APPROACH THE HERONS—IF DISTURBED, THEY MAY ABANDON THEIR NESTS.* Keep your eyes open for other marsh birds like American bitterns. Mallards, wood ducks, hooded mergansers, American black ducks, and Canada geese also nest in the area. Look for evidence of beavers, white-tailed deer, otters, fishers, and muskrats.

Directions: From Hillsborough, head north on Routes 202/9. Turn left onto Preston Road and go approximately 2 miles to a left turn onto Whitney Road. From Whitney Road, turn right onto Bog Road. Go about 3 miles to the dam site on the right side of the road.

Ownership: NHFG (603) 271-3211

Size: 469 acres   **Closest Town:** Hillsborough

34. SURRY MOUNTAIN LAKE

Description: The Ashuelot River provides the water for 265-acre Surry Mountain Lake. Visitors enjoy floating approximately four miles through undisturbed river habitat. The diverse upland portions of the area include old fields and a mixed woodland with oak, maple, and hemlock. Canoe and small boat access is available.

Viewing Information: The marshes at the upper end of the lake provide habitat for a variety of waterfowl. The old fields are an excellent place to hear and see American woodcocks and wild turkeys in the spring. Deer are a common sight in the area.

Directions: *From the junction of Routes 9 and 12 in Keene, travel north on Rte. 12 to the Maple Avenue exit. Turn right onto Maple Avenue. At the traffic light 0.9 mile later, continue straight. You are now on Rte. 12A. Proceed approximately 3 miles to Surry Mountain Recreation Area.*

Ownership: USACE (802) 886-8111

Size: 1,688 acres   **Closest Town:** Keene

35. DANIEL UPTON FOREST

Description: Except for a marshy pond in the southeast corner, the area is managed as a productive woodlot. Several trails cross the property, including a connector to the Monadnock-Sunapee Greenway.

Viewing Information: A short trail through sugar maple, beech, and hemlock woods leads to a marshy pond. During the spring and summer, a heron nesting colony is active here. *PLEASE DO NOT GO BEYOND THE VIEWING BLIND. HERONS ARE VERY SUSCEPTIBLE TO DISTURBANCE AND WILL ABANDON THEIR NESTS AND YOUNG.* Use the blind to increase your chances of seeing an abundance of other wildlife on and around the marsh, including wood ducks, beavers, Canada geese, red-winged blackbirds, tree swallows, belted kingfishers, beavers, deer, otters, and raccoons. A variety of warblers nests here; early summer is the best time to hear their songs.

Directions: *From the intersection of Routes 9 and 123 in Stoddard, go 0.5 mile west on Rte. 9. Turn right onto County Road. Proceed 0.8 mile and turn left onto another gravel road where there is a small parking area. Park well off the traveled portion of the road. There is a section of private land in the middle of the property. Please respect the privacy of the landowners.*

Ownership: SPNHF (603) 224-9945

Size: 163 acres   **Closest Town:** Stoddard

36. CHARLES L. PEIRCE WILDLIFE AND FOREST RESERVATION

Description: Visitors to the reservation can observe a number of land management practices and participate in a variety of recreational activities. The mixed woodlands of oak, maple, white pine, and hemlock provide an excellent example of this part of the state's forests. Some areas are intensively managed for timber and wildlife habitat and some areas remain wild. There are more than 10 miles of hiking trails and old roads. The 5-mile Trout-n-Bacon trail is of particular interest. A map and compass are recommended.

Viewing Information: In early summer, the woodlands teem with bird life. In some areas, you can hear the lovely songs of veeries, hermit thrushes, and wood thrushes. Solitary vireos, black-throated green warblers, and ovenbirds inhabit the area. The brooks and ponds are home to beavers, minks, and otters. Listen for spring peepers and wood frogs in the vernal pools in early spring. Watch for evidence of porcupines, deer, moose, and red squirrels.

Directions: *From Route 9 in Stoddard, go west on Rte. 123 for 2 miles. Turn right at the fire station, cross a bridge, and immediately bear right onto a dirt road. Use the small parking area after 0.4 mile if you are in a regular vehicle. If you have 4-wheel drive, continue another 0.6 mile to the parking area with the SPNHF sign. Or, bear left after the bridge, go 0.9 mile, and park along the road near the SPNHF sign. Trails leave from all three locations.*

Ownership: SPNHF (603) 224-9945

Size: 3,461 acres   **Closest Town:** Stoddard

Listen and look for wood frogs and other amphibians near ponds and vernal pools in early spring. The call of the wood frog sounds remarkably like a bunch of quacking ducks. They often breed before the ice is off the water. CHARLES H. WILLEY

UPLANDS

37. DEPIERREFEU-WILLARD POND WILDLIFE SANCTUARY

Description: At more than 1,000 acres, the dePierrefeu-Willard Pond Wildlife Sanctuary is the Audubon Society of New Hampshire's largest property. Additional gifts and easements and adjacent protected lands bring the entire protected area to well over 2,000 acres. Several outstanding features include 100-acre Willard Pond, Bald Mountain, and Goodhue Hill. Trails to the summits of the latter two provide views of North and South Pack Monadnock and the Grand Monadnock. The Tudor Trail affords wonderful opportunities to observe pond life. The Mill Pond Trail circles Hatch Mill Pond, where red maples and bog-loving shrubs can be found. A guide available at the sanctuary describes the trails.

Viewing Information: The sanctuary is home to a variety of wildlife. In summer, look for common loons, hooded mergansers, and wood ducks along the water's edge. The mixed deciduous and evergreen forest of hemlock, white pine, oak, and maple provides habitat for everything from gray squirrels to moose. During a late spring or summer walk, you are likely to hear ovenbirds, hermit thrushes, least flycatchers, and scarlet tanagers. Bald eagles visit periodically. Viewers delight in the antics of the young ravens and turkey vultures that nest and fledge in the sanctuary.

Directions: From Hancock Village, go west 3.7 miles on Route 123. Turn right onto a dirt road and go 1.6 miles, bearing left at the fork to the parking lot. The trails and pond are about 50 yards ahead. From the junction of Rtes. 123 and 9, go east on Rte. 123 for 3.3 miles, turn left onto the unmarked dirt road, and proceed the same way to the parking lot.

Ownership: ASNH 603 224-9909

Size: 1,000 acres   **Closest Town:** Hancock

Loons are very susceptible to human disturbance, predators, and fluctuating water levels, especially during the nesting season. Nest platforms were first used successfully in New Hampshire and are now used throughout the country. In summer, common loons are seen on lakes and ponds throughout the state. In winter they can be spotted along the coast.

38. MCCABE FOREST

Description: Two miles of Contoocook River frontage make this an excellent place to look for wildlife. The area offers a variety of habitats: old and mowed fields, brooks, and oak and white pine forests. There are trails throughout the property. The McCabe Forest is a designated wildlife habitat demonstration area; a trail guide explains what management actions have been implemented.

Viewing Information: Look for evidence of deer, foxes, and coyotes on the trails. Spring visitors may find woodcocks and ruffed grouse. The diverse habitats make it easy to see a variety of birds in the spring and summer, including indigo buntings, chestnut-sided warblers, American redstarts, Nashville warblers, and yellow warblers.

Directions: *From the intersection of Routes 31 and 202 in Antrim, head north on Rte. 202 for 0.2 mile. Turn right onto Elm Street and go 300 feet. Turn right into the parking area.*

Ownership: SPNHF (603) 224-9945

Size: 192 acres   **Closest Town:** Antrim

Most active at night, red foxes are found in a variety of habitats, including cities and suburbs. Even though red foxes are carnivores, they will eat almost anything, including berries, nuts, and grasses.
MARK S. WERNER

39. DEERING WILDLIFE SANCTUARY

Description: The premier property of the Audubon Society of New Hampshire, this sanctuary provides excellent examples of active habitat management. Once farmed, the area has a mixed white pine and oak woodlands, an old orchard, and an artificial pond created by a dam on Smith Brook. A trail guide is available.

Viewing Information: The sanctuary's diverse habitat types provide opportunities to see a variety of wildlife. Downy and hairy woodpeckers, raccoons, and porcupines find refuge in snags. Look for scarlet tanagers, indigo buntings, veeries, wood thrushes, and hermit thrushes. Open areas with meadowsweet and raspberries are a haven for butterflies and other nectar-loving insects. At the approach to the pond, notice evidence of beaver activity. Otters and minks also make their homes here. The pond is a place to see red-winged blackbirds; wood ducks and hooded mergansers use the pond's artificial nesting boxes; and green and great blue herons find plenty of food here. In summer, the water's edge is alive with green frogs and bullfrogs. A myriad of waterfowl and other migrating birds such as ospreys use the pond as a stopover.

Directions: *From the light in the center of Hillsborough (Routes 202 and 9) go south on Rte. 149. Travel 1 mile, then turn left onto Clement Hill Road. Go 1.5 miles and turn right at the sign. The first parking area is 0.3 mile ahead on the right.*

Ownership: ASNH (603) 224-9909

Size: 485 acres   **Closest Town:** Hillsborough

Choruses of spring peepers are the traditional signal that winter is over. Their peep is among the louder known animal sounds, equivalent in noise level to the roar of a motorcycle 25 feet away.

Expert tree climbers, raccoons prefer fairly mature hardwood areas and generally nest in hollow trees. They eat a wide variety of foods. MARK & SUE WERNER

40. PERKINS POND WILDLIFE MANAGEMENT AREA

Description: Perkins Pond is surrounded by a variety of habitats including open marsh, old fields, and mixed woodlands. Small boats and canoes can be launched from the area adjacent to the dam. Several pull-offs along the road provide viewing opportunities.

Viewing Information: Canada geese, American black ducks, wood ducks, and hooded mergansers nest on the pond. Wading birds such as great blue herons, green herons, and American bitterns fish in the shallows and along the marsh. Mammals that use the area include beavers, muskrats, and white-tailed deer.

Directions: *From the junction of Routes 114 and 77 in South Weare, follow Rte. 114 west toward Hillsborough for 1.9 miles. The pond and marsh lie on the south side of the road.*

Ownership: NHFG (603) 271-3211

Size: 308 acres   **Closest Town:** South Weare

41. WANTASTIQUET STATE FOREST AND MADAME SHERI FOREST

Description: Two natural communities come together in this area, making it one of the most ecologically significant sites in the state. Here, the northern New England acidic rocky summit community meets the southern New England acidic talus forest. The influence of the Connecticut River increases the area's diversity. Take a walk in the woods through sycamores, cottonwoods, mountain laurels, hemlocks, and sugar maples. The interior old roads allow visitors to walk along the Connecticut River to the summit of Wantastiquet Mountain. The properties are closed to wheeled vehicles.

Viewing Information: The Connecticut River serves as a travel corridor for more than a hundred different kinds of birds. In late April and early May, thousands of warblers pass through the area on their way north. Late summer is a good time to view a variety of shorebirds. Look for evidence of mammals such as otters, minks, fishers, and red and gray squirrels.

Directions: *From Route 9 just east of the bridge into Vermont, turn south onto Mountain Road. Follow Mountain Road for 1.1 miles to its end. From here, you can access the Wantastiquet State Forest. To enter through Madame Sheri Forest, turn left from Mountain Road onto Gulf Road at 0.1 mile. Bear left at the fork and continue for 2.5 miles. Park at the red SPNHF gate on the right side of Gulf Road.*

Ownership: DRED—Division of Forests and Lands (603) 271-3456 and SPNHF (603) 224-9945

Size: Wantastiquet State Forest: 1,011 acres; Madame Sheri Forest: 488 acres.
Closest Town: Hinsdale

Description: Located in New Hampshire's largest state park, the scenic rocky-shore pond can only be reached on foot. The Kilburn Pond loop trail is a little more than 5 miles long (there is also a shorter route); it leads through a typical southern New Hampshire woods of hemlock, oak, and white pine. The area was once heavily settled and farmed; remnants of stone walls reveal the impact humans had on the land. The pond has a small bog at its northern end and an extended marsh to the south.

Viewing Information: Pisgah's size makes it a place where wildlife has been minimally disturbed. Visitors can find evidence of fishers, otters, beavers, muskrats, and minks. The amount of continuous forest provides ideal habitat for hermit thrushes, veeries, wood thrushes, and ovenbirds. Early on spring mornings, vireos, tanagers, and warblers fill the air with sound. Depending on the time of year, you can see great blue herons, common yellowthroats, and, occasionally, American black ducks and wood ducks.

Directions: *From Keene, drive 11 miles west on Route 9 and turn south onto Rte. 63. After about 4.4 miles, turn left into a gravel parking area signed Pisgah State Park, Kilburn Road Trailhead.*

Ownership: DRED—Division of Parks and Recreation (603) 271-3556, DRED—Division of Forests and Lands (603) 271-3456

Size: 13,000 acres   **Closest Town:** Winchester

UPLANDS

Bobcats are elusive predators that prefer rocky, wild country. When hunting, they creep along from cover to cover until they are close enough to pounce on their prey. MARK & SUE WERNER

43. EDWARD MACDOWELL LAKE

Description: A dam forms a small lake here, with access to a large marsh and Nubanusit Brook. A picnic area and canoe launch make this a nice place to spend an afternoon. The upland areas are representative of the typical mixed forests found in this part of the state. During the summer months, a naturalist conducts interpretive programs

Viewing Information: Observe the wetland animals by walking the road along the edge of the lake or going out in a canoe. Don't forget to look for turtles and frogs. In spring and summer, look and listen for common yellowthroats and tree swallows. You may get a glimpse of a northern harrier or hear an American bittern. Canada geese and American black ducks nest here. In the fall, look for migrating waterfowl. Early evening is a great time to observe bats in action.

Directions: *From the junction of Routes 101 and 202 in Peterborough, head west on Rte. 101 for 2.3 miles. Turn left on Union Street and drive 0.6 mile. Turn left on Wilder Street and follow it to the dam and recreation area.*

Ownership: USACE (603) 924-3431

Size: 1,194 acres　　**Closest Town:** Peterborough

Canada geese travel in a V-formation, announcing their approach by musical honking or barking. It is difficult to tell the male from the female. During courtship, listen for the low "ahonk" call of the male and and the higher "hink" call of the female. CHARLES H. WILLEY

Description: The Deland Forest is an excellent place to see examples of forestry practices both past and present. The management efforts have created a working forest that takes into consideration wildlife, aesthetics, and economic value. There are three walking trails; an accompanying brochure is available.

Viewing Information: Management practices have encouraged a diversity of wildlife in the forest. Look for woodpeckers, black-and-white warblers, brown creepers, and nuthatches. You may find black-capped chickadees, crossbills, and pine grosbeaks feeding on the seeds of white pine cones. Be on the lookout for red squirrels and chipmunks. Along the Burnham Brook Trail, keep your eyes open for signs of porcupines, otters, snowshoe hares, deer, and moose. The Beaver Lodge Trail takes you along the South Branch of the Piscataquog River. Evidence of beaver activity abounds, including old dams and a lodge. As you walk along the banks, examine holes for signs of beavers, minks, and otters.

Directions: *On Route 13, just south of the junction of Routes 77 and 13, turn right on Old Coach Road. Go 3 miles and turn south on Butterfield Mill Road (dirt). Follow this road for about 1.3 miles until you see the sign and parking area.*

Ownership: The New England Forestry Foundation owns the property and SPNHF oversees the activities as set forth by a conservation easement. ASNH designed and built the nature trails. (603) 224-9945

Size: 700 acres   **Closest Town:** New Boston

UPLANDS

Snowshoe hares provide an excellent example of protective coloration: they are brown in the summer and turn white as autumn changes to winter. Snowshoe hares spend their entire lives traversing the same small area, a piece of ground no more than thirty acres.

REGION 3—SOUTHERN NEW HAMPSHIRE COASTAL PLAIN AND HILLS

This section of New Hampshire has been heavily influenced by its geologic history, the Atlantic Ocean, and human land use. Two unique geologic features of the area are the circular-shaped Ossipee Range and the Pawtuckaway Mountains, both formed by the collapse of ancient volcanoes. This area includes the state's largest natural lakes, hills, and ridges, as well as wetlands carved and formed by the last glacier over 10,000 years ago. The Merrimack River valley is filled with glacial outwash and glacial lake deposits. The Seabrook-Hampton and Great Bay estuaries dramatically increase the amount of shoreline touched by salt water. The coastline was the first part of New Hampshire to be settled; only small remnants of the coastal dune communities remain.

Oak, maple, and white pine create a tapestry on the landscape, with areas of sandy soils supporting the rarer pitch pine and scrub oak communities. Once heavily farmed, the southern coastal plains and hills are seeing urban and suburban development today. The bird and mammal life is varied: visitors can see harbor seals, common terns, white-tailed deer, wild turkeys, and rare moths and butterflies.

The coast of New Hampshire contains a wide diversity of marine habitats, including salt marshes, sandy beaches, and rocky ledges. The Great Bay estuary is a refuge for twenty-three species of threatened or endangered animals and plants. GEORGE WUERTHNER

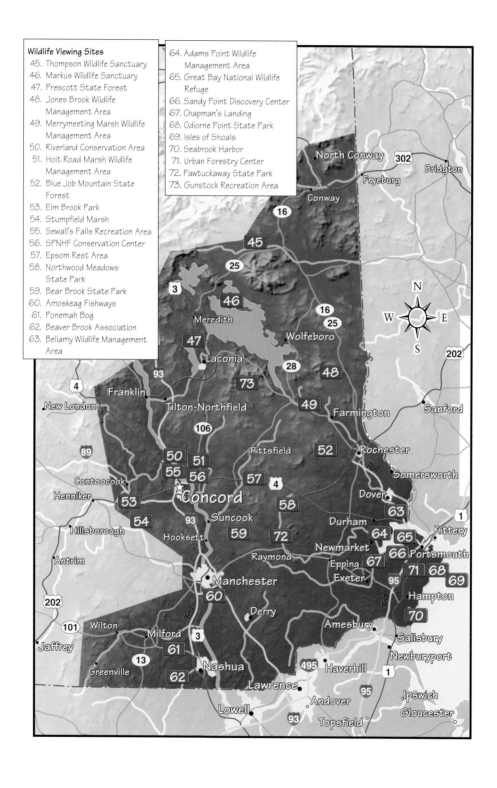

Wildlife Viewing Sites

45. Thompson Wildlife Sanctuary
46. Markus Wildlife Sanctuary
47. Prescott State Forest
48. Jones Brook Wildlife Management Area
49. Merrymeeting Marsh Wildlife Management Area
50. Riverland Conservation Area
51. Hoit Road Marsh Wildlife Management Area
52. Blue Job Mountain State Forest
53. Elm Brook Park
54. Stumpfield Marsh
55. Sewall's Falls Recreation Area
56. SPNHF Conservation Center
57. Epsom Rest Area
58. Northwood Meadows State Park
59. Bear Brook State Park
60. Amoskeag Fishways
61. Ponemah Bog
62. Beaver Brook Association
63. Bellamy Wildlife Management Area

64. Adams Point Wildlife Management Area
65. Great Bay National Wildlife Refuge
66. Sandy Point Discovery Center
67. Chapman's Landing
68. Odiorne Point State Park
69. Isles of Shoals
70. Seabrook Harbor
71. Urban Forestry Center
72. Pawtuckaway State Park
73. Gunstock Recreation Area

OSPREY

ATLANTIC WHITE CEDAR

SEASIDE GOLDENROD

NEW ENGLAND COTTONTAIL

GREEN DARNER DRAGONFLY

EASTERN RIBBON SNAKE

GREATER YELLOWLEGS

NORTHERN LEOPARD FROG

MUMMICHOG

Coastal New Hampshire

Though New Hampshire's coastline is short, it contains a wide diversity of marine habitats, including the Great Bay and Seabrook-Hampton estuaries, salt marshes, sandy beaches, and rock ledges. The diversity of animals is illustrated by more than 350 different kinds of invertebrates found here. Special adaptations allow

DOUBLE-CRESTED CORMORANT

HARBOR SEAL

GLASSWORT

SNOWY EGRET

HORSESHOE CRAB

CORD GRASS

GREEN CRAB

STRIPED BASS

wildlife to live where there are daily fluctuations of tides and changes in salinity. When visiting the coast there are always things to observe, whether it is scanning the mudflats for shorebirds or staring into tidepools watching barnacles as they filter feed.

Description: A gift from Charles G. Thompson to the Audubon Society, the sanctuary has a marsh surrounded by tamaracks and an upland area, both crowded with bird and animal life. A trail guide is available.

Viewing Information: A series of beaver impoundments on Atwood Brook created the marsh. A trail leads across it to an upland area of hardwoods and evergreens; the trail is wheelchair accessible for about 350 yards. The open area around the marsh affords spectacular views of the Sandwich Range to the north and of the circular dike of the Ossipee Mountains to the east. Great blue herons, red-winged blackbirds, belted kingfishers, eastern kingbirds, and northern waterthrushes thrive on the marsh. Visitors have seen tree swallows, wood ducks, hooded mergansers, northern harriers, common snipes, and even elusive Virginia rails. Don't be surprised to hear a sound like failed plumbing: it's a bittern calling from a hidden spot. Moose and deer can be seen around the marsh in spring and summer, especially in the early morning or late evening hours. Watch for foxes and otters or their evidence on the trail. As it moves into the forest, the trail passes through tamarack, fern, sweetgale, Juneberry, and wild rose. On the drier upland soil, a mixture of white pine, hemlock, birch, and maple provides homes for black-throated blue warblers, red-eyed vireos, white-breasted nuthatches, and ruffed grouse. A trail marked in yellow goes by a large glacial erratic.

Directions: *From the junction of Routes 25 and 113, 1.2 miles west of South Tamworth, go north on Rte. 113 toward North Sandwich. After 2.7 miles, look for the ASNH sanctuary sign on the left. There is parking for two cars.*

Ownership: ASNH (603) 224-9909

Size: 200 acres   **Closest Town:** North Sandwich

Binoculars and spotting scopes help bridge the distance between you and wildlife. Binoculars come in a variety of sizes including 7 x 35, 8 x 40, and 10 x 50. The first number refers to how large the animal will be magnified compared to seeing it with the unaided eye. The second number tells you the lens diameter, which affects how much light will enter the lens.

Description: On the northeastern shore of Lake Winnipesaukee, the sanctuary encompasses upland forests, marshes, a pond, clear-running streams, and more than five thousand feet of undeveloped shoreline. The property is leased from the Markus Foundation by the Audubon Society of New Hampshire and serves as the new headquarters of the Loon Preservation Committee.

Viewing Information: Two trails explore the area. The Forest Walk is a short, easy loop; use it to observe woodland birds such as ovenbirds, red-eyed vireos, chickadees, and woodpeckers. Depending upon the season and the time of day, you may see deer, moose, beavers, and other wildlife. The Loon Nest Trail follows Halfway Brook toward the lakeshore. It continues along the shoreline, eventually moving slightly uphill. At the fork in the trail, go right. Just beyond where the trail "squeezes" between two granite boulders is the best place to view the sanctuary's loon nest.

Directions: *Take Route 25 to Moultonborough. At Moultonborough Central School, turn right onto Blake Road. Go 1 mile to the road's end and turn right onto Lees Mills Road. The sanctuary and Loon Center are on the left.*

Ownership: Markus Foundation: leased by ASNH and Loon Preservation Committee (603) 476-LOON

Size: 200 acres   **Closest Town:** Moultonborough

COASTAL

The cry of the common loon symbolizes wilderness for many people. Loons have four basic calls that they use to communicate with each other: wail, yodel, tremolo, and hoot. Loons are extremely sensitive to the presence of people; keep your distance. JOHN H. GAVIN

47. PRESCOTT STATE FOREST

Description: Old fields, wetlands, and woods provide habitat for a variety of species. There is an old apple orchard on the property.

Viewing Information: This is a good place to find field-loving songbirds such as bobolinks, tree swallows, field sparrows, and indigo buntings in the late spring and summer. Northern orioles, chestnut-sided warblers, American red-starts, and rose-breasted grosbeaks live here. The old apple orchard attracts white-tailed deer, ruffed grouse, coyotes, and foxes. In the wetland area, look for evidence of minks and muskrats and listen for common yellowthroats.

Directions: *From Route 3 in Laconia, go north on Parade Road for 4.4 miles. At the south end of the large hayfield, turn left into a dirt driveway. Park along the edge of the circular drive. From Rte. 104 in Meredith, travel south on Parade Road for 4 miles and turn right into the dirt driveway.*

Ownership: DRED—Division of Forests and Lands (603) 271-3456

Size: 116 acres   **Closest Town:** Laconia

48. JONES BROOK WILDLIFE MANAGEMENT AREA

Description: The landscape here is diverse, with steep, rocky sections; several ponds (including a manmade one); a small wetland; and some relatively flat sections covered with white pine, hemlock, and areas of hardwoods. The management area is accessible by foot.

Viewing Information: As you walk through the area, be on the lookout for signs of bears, moose, white-tailed deer, and snowshoe hares. Don't be surprised if you are scolded by chipmunks and squirrels. Spring is a good time to find American woodcocks and ruffed grouse. A wide variety of songbirds nests on the property.

Directions: *From Middleton Corners, go north on King's Highway for 2.5 miles to the Strafford/Carroll county line. Continue for another 0.5 mile; on the right, you will see a dirt road with a gate. Parking is limited to three cars.*

Ownership: NHFG (603) 271-3211

Size: 1,493 acres   **Closest Town:** Wolfeboro

49. MERRYMEETING MARSH WILDLIFE MANAGEMENT AREA

Description: This large freshwater marsh is surrounded by oak and white pine woodlands. Several pull-offs allow viewing from the road, and there is a boat launch area where you can put in your canoe.

Viewing Information: A canoe is helpful in exploring this site to its fullest. On the uplands around the marsh, look and listen for yellow-rumped warblers, scarlet tanagers, and song sparrows. Visitors can find evidence of muskrats and beavers, and can occasionally see a white-tailed deer. Great blue herons, wood ducks, eastern kingbirds, tree and rough-winged swallows, and marsh wrens use the marsh. In summer, watch for American black ducks, mallards, hooded mergansers, and Canada geese. During fall migration, add blue- and green-winged teal, ring-necked ducks, and common mergansers.

Directions: *From the intersection of Routes 11 and 28 (Alton Traffic Circle), head east on Route 11. Proceed approximately 2.4 miles; Merrymeeting Marsh Boat Ramp is on the right side of Rte. 11.*

Ownership: NHFG (603) 271-3211

Size: 389 acres   **Closest Town:** New Durham

COASTAL

Look for the white band across the tip of the tail to help identify eastern kingbirds. These birds have favorite perches from which they catch flying insects. Sometimes they seem to fly on quivering wing tips. JOHN H. GAVIN

50. RIVERLAND CONSERVATION AREA

Description: The Merrimack River shaped this land and continues to be a major influence on it. The land includes river frontage, two oxbow ponds, wetlands, fields, and woods. The area has several trails, including a boardwalk and a viewing platform at one of the oxbow ponds. A parking area provides canoe and rowboat access to the pond. There is a piece of private land in the middle of the area; please be respectful of the landowner's privacy.

Viewing Information: During spring warbler migration in May, use the area to view birds that nest farther north. In the summer, the area is home to bank and rough-winged swallows; eastern bluebirds; field, swamp, and song sparrows; great blue herons; red-tailed hawks; chestnut-sided warblers; and rufous-sided towhees. Watch for evidence of beavers and otters, and for the abundant turtles and frogs. Along the river, look for signs that raccoons have been feeding on the freshwater mussels. The ponds and river support a variety of fish, including largemouth and smallmouth bass, sunfish, horned pout, and pickerel.

Directions: *Take exit 17 off Interstate 93. Head west on Route 4 for 0.2 mile. Turn right on Old Boyce Road. Keep left at the fork, veering onto Riverland Road. Follow Riverland Road to Oxbow Pond Road. The parking area is at the end of Oxbow Pond Road.*

Ownership: Town of Canterbury (603) 783-4866

Size: 90 acres   **Closest Town:** Canterbury

Birds use calls to communicate with others of the same kind, usually through short bursts of sharp, high-pitched notes. They use songs to proclaim their identity and establish a territory. Songs tend to be longer, with a recognizable melody or pattern, and are generally sung by males.

51. HOIT ROAD MARSH WILDLIFE MANAGEMENT AREA AND THE RILEY LOT

Description: Created by a dam, the marsh has a large pond area and is surrounded by oak and white pine uplands.

Viewing Information: Located within 7 miles of the state capital, this area is a good place to see wildlife. During the fall, visitors can see American black ducks, mallards, green-winged teal, and Canada geese. In the spring and early summer, wood ducks and hooded mergansers use the wood duck nest boxes. Look for wading birds, such as green and great blue herons, along the marsh edges. Tree swallows, belted kingfishers, and common yellowthroats are abundant in the summer. On the uplands, listen for ovenbirds and veeries. You may see moose, deer, otters, and beavers. An interpretive trail beginning on the Riley Lot explains the different types of habitat management taking place here.

Directions: *Take exit 17 off Interstate 93. Follow Hoit Road east for 3 miles. The marsh borders the north side of the road. Parking is available on the south side of the road opposite the dam as well as 250 yards farther east at the Riley Lot.*

Ownership: Hoit Marsh: NHFG; the Riley Lot: City of Concord (603) 271-3211

Size: 209 acres   **Closest Town:** Concord

COASTAL

Wetlands, like this one at Hoit Road Marsh WMA, provide habitat during some part of the year for over one-third of New Hampshire's wildlife. NEW HAMPSHIRE FISH & GAME DEPARTMENT

Description: A fire tower atop a small mountain offers panoramic views of the eastern part of the state.

Viewing Information: The best time to visit Blue Job Mountain is during the fall hawk migration. As many as 800 broad-winged hawks have been seen in one day between September 15 and 20. A short, easy uphill climb brings you to the fire tower; the trail passes through an old blueberry field, now growing in with young aspen. In the spring and early summer, chestnut-sided warblers and rufous-sided towhees are abundant. A trail leads from the fire tower to Little Blue Job Mountain, which is covered in blueberry bushes. When the berries are ripe, the area hosts a variety of wildlife, including foxes and bears.

Directions: From Rochester, drive west on Route 202A. Two miles past Meaderboro Corner, take Crown Point Road, which bears right. Continue for 5.5 miles, past farmland and woods. Look for the parking area on the right; it is on private property, across from a farmhouse. The trail begins to the left of the parking area, on private land. It is not marked with a sign, but is well worn.

Ownership: DRED—Division of Forests and Lands (603) 271-3456

Size: 284 acres   **Closest Town:** Rochester

Active year-round in pine or spruce-fir forests, red squirrels are sometimes called "boomers" or "fairy diddles." Their scolding trill lets all the other forest creatures know if there is potential danger, like humans, in the forest. KEVIN A. BYRON

53. ELM BROOK PARK

Description: On the shore of the Hopkinton Reservoir, this park is part of the flood control project for the Contoocook River. The park has a variety of landscapes—fields, marshes, lakeshore, and mixed forests. Visitor facilities include a barrier-free wildlife viewing platform. Interpretive programs are offered during the summer.

Viewing Information: A variety of wildlife use the park, including white-tailed deer, beavers, muskrats, minks, otters, raccoons, and an occasional moose. Visitors often see raptors, such as red-tailed hawks and kestrels. Look for great blue herons and other shorebirds by the lake. In summer, waterfowl use the reservoir for nesting, and their numbers increase during fall migration. Watch for tree swallows, bluebirds, savannah sparrows, northern bobwhites, and other field-loving songbirds during the summer.

Directions: *Take exit 6 off Interstate 89 North. At the top of the ramp, turn left onto Route 127. Stay on Rte. 127 for 1.1 miles. Turn left on the park entrance road, which is a gravel road with a yellow gate. This road will take you directly to the park. From Rtes. 202/9, take Rte. 127 north. Stay on Rte. 127 for 2.3 miles; the park entrance road will be on the right.*

Ownership: USACE (603) 746-3601

Size: 8,245 acres   **Closest Town:** Hopkinton

COASTAL

Neotropical migrants are birds that make the long migratory flight from one continent to another. Many of the more than seventy neotropical migrants that breed in New Hampshire have experienced population declines. New Hampshire is taking part in an international effort called Partners in Flight, which seeks to protect species whose numbers are declining as well as ecosystems that are being threatened.

54. STUMPFIELD MARSH

Description: Formed by the "back-up" from the Hopkinton-Everett Flood Control project, Stumpfield Marsh is an area of open water and standing snags.

Viewing Information: Visitors to the marsh can view a great blue heron rookery from spring through July. DO NOT ATTEMPT TO APPROACH THE BIRDS. HERONS MAY ABANDON NEST SITES IF DISTURBED. A variety of waterfowl species also nest here, including wood ducks, American black ducks, hooded mergansers, and green-winged teal. Other summer residents include Virginia rails, tree swallows, great crested flycatchers, and belted kingfishers. This is a good spot to look for turtles. White-tailed deer use the area during three seasons of the year; watch for them in the early morning or late evening.

Directions: *From Interstate 89, go south on Routes 202/9. Turn left onto Stumpfield Road and go 0.7 mile to a dirt road on the right with a yellow gate at its entrance. Follow the road 0.2 mile to Stumpfield Marsh.*

Ownership: DRED—Division of Forests and Lands under a management agreement with USACE (603) 271-3456

Size: 175 acres   **Closest Town:** Hopkinton

55. SEWALL'S FALLS RECREATION AREA

Description: The wild and scenic corridor of the Merrimack River cuts through the land here just as it did two hundred years ago. Located in the state capital, Sewall's Falls Recreation Area provides trails and river access. The north end of the area has a boat launch; at the south end, a small park sits among the remains of an old power generating facility.

Viewing Information: A walk along the river's edge reveals many of the secrets of this special place. Great blue herons and ospreys feed here. Be on the lookout for spotted sandpipers, tree and bank swallows, and belted kingfishers; watch for evidence of minks, otters, and raccoons. This section of the river provides important habitat for Atlantic salmon and freshwater mussels.

Directions: *The north end of the recreation area is accessed from Sewall's Falls Road. Take exit 17 off Interstate 93. Head east on Hoit Road. Turn right on Mountain Road and drive approximately 1 mile, then turn right on Sewall's Falls Road. The entrance to the parking area is on the left, shortly after you cross a bridge.*

Ownership: NHFG (603) 271-3211

Size: 136 acres   **Closest Town:** Concord

Great blue herons silently stalk fish and frogs, spearing them with their long, sharp bills. In flight the neck is usually folded back, the long legs trail behind, and the broad wings flap slowly and deliberately. CHARLES H. WILLEY

56. SPNHF CONSERVATION CENTER/MERRIMACK RIVER OUTDOOR EDUCATION AND CONSERVATION AREA

Description: The conservation area provides a fine example of Merrimack River bluff and floodplain landscapes. The passive solar headquarters of the SPNHF (Society for the Protection of New Hampshire Forest) is at the top of the bluff, surrounded by oak, white pine, and pitch pine forest. Educational activities are conducted on this site.

Viewing Information: In late April and early May, birders walk the trails to see the array of warblers that use the river corridor. In summer, look for raptors, including red-tailed hawks, kestrels, and ospreys; you may see a bald eagle in the winter. Bank and rough-winged swallows, brown thrashers, and rufous-sided towhees are common sights in the summer months. Watch for American black ducks, mallards, and ring-necked ducks along the river. Pileated woodpeckers leave evidence of their visits on the bluff. Look for signs of deer, beavers, and other mammals.

Directions: *From Interstate 93 in Concord, go east on I-393 to exit 2. Turn right and go 1.1 miles, then turn left onto Portsmouth Street. The Conservation Center's driveway is 0.2 mile on the left; or, continue an additional 0.2 mile to the trail parking lot on the left.*

Ownership: SPNHF (603) 224-9945

Size: 95 acres   **Closest Town:** Concord

The Karner blue butterfly, limited in New England to the Concord Pine Barrens, relies on wild lupine as an exclusive food source for part of its life cycle. Wild lupine needs fire to maintain the open conditions it requires. For thousands of years, large areas of southern New Hampshire experienced frequent fires. This resulted in a mosaic of young and old pitch pine and scrub oak woodlands. Today, development has confined and fragmented the pine barrens, and fire suppression has reduced the necessary regeneration. As a result, Karner blue populations have dwindled.

57. EPSOM REST AREA

Description: The best wildlife viewing can sometimes be right next to a perfect stopping place. The pond, marsh, and woods that surround the Epsom rest area almost always offer something of interest.

Viewing Information: In the spring, the marsh is alive with birds on their way north. Canada geese, American black ducks, mallards, and green-winged teal stop here to rest and feed. Red-winged blackbirds flash their colors as they set up nesting territories. Listen carefully for spring peeper calls in the spring and green frog and bullfrog calls in the summer. Also in the summer, watch for great blue herons wading in the shallows. You may even see a muskrat or a beaver swimming along the water's edge.

Directions: From the Epsom traffic circle head west on Route 4 for 2.5 miles. The rest area is on the south side of the highway.

Ownership: New Hampshire Department of Transportation (603) 736-4974

Size: 10 acres   **Closest Town:** Epsom

58. NORTHWOOD MEADOWS STATE PARK

Description: The headwaters of the Lamprey River are at Northwood Meadows. The park offers ponds and wetlands surrounded by oak and white pine forests. Universally accessible trails lead to areas around the ponds, with more under development. Northwood Meadows abuts an additional 900 acres of conservation land.

Viewing Information: During the summer you can expect to see or hear a wide variety of birds, including eastern wood-pewees, least and great crested flycatchers, tufted titmice, brown creepers, veeries, hermit thrushes, common yellowthroats, scarlet tanagers, swamp sparrows, and blue-gray gnatcatchers. Listen for downy, hairy, and pileated woodpeckers. While exploring, you may find evidence of beavers, white-tailed deer, and otters. Wood ducks, hooded mergansers, and American black ducks use the ponds. During fall migration, waterfowl stop at the ponds and adjacent wetlands to rest and feed.

Directions: The park entrance is on Route 4 in Northwood, 0.5 mile east of the town hall.

Ownership: DRED—Division of Parks and Recreation (603) 271-3556

Size: 665 acres   **Closest Town:** Northwood

59. BEAR BROOK STATE PARK

Description: Bear Brook is a large, popular park with a varied landscape near Concord and Manchester. Oak and white pine forests surround ponds, marshes, and rocky outcroppings. The park offers a full complement of facilities.

Viewing Information: The best places to see wildlife are the areas around the ponds and marshes. Beavers are active at several locations. The large amount of continuous forest makes this a good place to hear veeries, hermit thrushes, wood thrushes, and ovenbirds in the late spring and summer. Look for wood ducks, mallards, American black ducks, and hooded mergansers on the more remote marshes and ponds.

Directions: *From Route 28 in Allenstown, turn east onto Deerfield Road and follow signs to the park. The park has several different areas; those of special interest include Spruce Pond, Smith Pond, Hayes Marsh, and Hall Mountain Marsh.*

Ownership: DRED—Division of Parks (603) 271-3556

Size: 9,585 acres   **Closest Town:** Suncook

Wood ducks require cavities for nesting. Male wood ducks are often considered the most beautiful North American duck. Female wood ducks, however, blend into their surroundings. CHARLES H. WILLEY

Description: Operated under a unique public/private partnership, which includes Public Service of New Hampshire, New Hampshire Fish and Game, the Audubon Society of New Hampshire, and the U.S. Fish and Wildlife Service, this environmental education center is open year-round. A fish ladder operates from late April through mid-June as part of the Atlantic salmon and American shad restoration program. The center is located on the Merrimack River at a hydro-power generating facility. It offers a full spectrum of educational programs and exhibits about the Merrimack River.

Viewing Information: From late April to mid-June, visitors have a unique opportunity to watch both resident and anadromous fish use the fish ladder. An aquarium allows you to see a variety of fish at any time of year. The Amoskeag Fishways site provides excellent opportunities to see bald eagles during the winter. Watch for a variety of ducks such as common goldeneyes, American black ducks, mallards, and mergansers in the open water below the dam. Landscaping for wildlife has made the site attractive to hummingbirds, butterflies, and a wide variety of songbirds. During the spring warbler migration, thousands of birds pass through the area on their way up the Merrimack River corridor. Summer residents include scarlet tanagers, red-eyed vireos, mockingbirds, catbirds, rose-breasted grosbeaks, Baltimore orioles, and belted kingfishers.

Directions: *From Route 3 (Daniel Webster Highway), take exit 6, Amoskeag Bridge. Turn right on Fletcher Street just past the Inn at Amoskeag.*

Ownership: Public Service of New Hampshire (603) 626-FISH

Size: 3 acres   **Closest Town:** Manchester

COASTAL

Many animals rely on sound to communicate among themselves and to alert each other to danger. Be careful about the sounds you make. The secret of a successful wildlife watcher is to become part of the natural scene. Find a dry, warm place to sit, lean back, and relax. The less movement you make and the longer you sit there, the more likely you are to see something.

Description: The sanctuary features a 3-acre pond surrounded by a floating sphagnum mat, all encircled by oak and pitch pine woods. The bog is in a kettle hole created by the retreat of the glaciers. Classic bog plants such as leatherleaf, bog laurel, and tamarack grow here. Visit in mid-May to see a spectacular display of Rhodora. You can also find insect-eating plants: pitcher plants, sundews, and bladderworts. A trail, a boardwalk, and a viewing platform allow you to get a closeup view of life in the bog, but be prepared for wet footing. A trail guide is available.

Viewing Information: Bird life in the sanctuary includes rufous-sided towhees, blue jays, tree swallows, common yellowthroats, mourning and Canada warblers, and song sparrows. Watch for green herons and other waterfowl, woodpeckers, and belted kingfishers. Occasionally, muskrats make their home in the bog. You can sometimes find signs of red foxes, raccoons, and other visitors from the nearby woods.

Directions: *From the junction of Routes 101 and 101A, go east on Rte. 101A for about 0.5 mile, then turn left onto Rte. 122. Take Stearns Road on your right, and go about 1.6 miles. Turn south onto Rhodora Drive and go straight ahead to park for the sanctuary.*

Ownership: ASNH (603) 224-9909

Size: 75 acres   **Closest Town:** Milford

Bog-loving pitcher plants are one of the better known carnivorous plants. They attract insects, their primary food source, to their innocent looking vase. Insects supplement the plants' nitrogen.
CHARLES H. WILLEY

62. BEAVER BROOK ASSOCIATION

Description: The Beaver Brook Association founders had genuine foresight when they began their land protection efforts more than thirty years ago: they chose what is now one of the fastest growing areas of New Hampshire. Their land encompasses fields, ponds, wetlands, and woods, and is overlaid with 35 miles of trails. Much of the land serves as a forestry and wildlife management demonstration area. The association offers extensive education programs for youth and adults.

Viewing Information: More than 125 species of birds have been recorded in the area. The land supports an abundance of small mammals such as squirrels, chipmunks, and rabbits, and provides important habitat components for white-tailed deer. Beavers are active in the wetlands, ponds, and brooks.

Directions: To reach Beaver Brook Association lands, take Route 122 south from Hollis. Turn right onto Ridge Road and drive approximately 1 mile. A parking area and the main facility are on the right. Five parking areas in all provide access to the land.

Ownership: Beaver Brook Association (603) 465-7787

Size: 2,000 acres   **Closest Town:** Hollis

63. BELLAMY WILDLIFE MANAGEMENT AREA

Description: The property is a combination of agricultural land, estuarine and freshwater wetlands, and wooded river banks. Just a short distance away are a 30-acre Audubon Society of New Hampshire sanctuary and city conservation land in Dover.

Viewing Information: In fall and winter, Bellamy is a significant feeding and resting area for migrating waterfowl, including American black ducks, mallards, and Canada geese. Watch for bald eagles in the winter. The agricultural land provides habitat for many field-dependent songbirds such as bobolinks, indigo buntings, and field sparrows. Summer brings red-tailed hawks and ospreys. You may find evidence of white-tailed deer, snowshoe hares, cottontail rabbits, coyotes, and bobcats.

Directions: On Route 4, approximately 2.2 miles east of the junction of Rtes. 4 and 108, turn left on Back River Road. Follow this for approximately 0.7 mile. Turn right on Rabbit Road, go 0.1 mile, and turn right onto Garrison Road. Proceed approximately 300 feet to the dirt roadway and parking area.

Ownership: NHFG (603) 271-3211

Size: 400 acres   **Closest Town:** Dover

Description: Once an island, Adams Point is now a peninsula separating Great Bay from Little Bay. The area is a mixture of old field, salt marsh, and oak/hemlock/white pine forest. At low tide, you can smell the sea and explore the mudflats and rocky beaches. Adams Point has supported a farm, a hotel, a brickyard, and a shipyard over the years; evidence of these can still be found. The only buildings now on the site belong to the nationally known Jackson Estuarine Research Laboratory. A trail encircles the point.

Viewing Information: This is the best place on Great Bay to view bald eagles in the winter; use the platform near the parking area. Adams Point also provides great vantage points from which to observe a variety of waterfowl and shorebirds. In summer, you may see snowy egrets, great blue herons, glossy ibises, and greater yellowlegs. The marsh and field areas provide nesting and forage for many songbirds, including song sparrows, bobolinks, and a variety of warblers. From autumn through spring, watch for greater scaup, Canada geese, common goldeneyes, mallards, American black ducks, buffleheads, and red-breasted mergansers. Owls, mice, voles, raccoons, white-tailed deer, ruffed grouse, muskrats, chipmunks, squirrels, rabbits, coyotes, and foxes reside in the forest, fields, and stone walls.

Directions: *From Durham, take Route 108 south for 0.4 mile. Turn left on Durham Point Road. Go 3.5 miles and turn left at signs for Adams Point Road. Proceed to the parking lot at the end of the road.*

Ownership: NHFG (603) 868-1095

Size: 82 acres   **Closest Town:** Durham

Winter is a hard time for bald eagles. When food is hard to find and the air is cold, they must conserve energy and body heat. Flushing eagles from their roosting trees causes them to waste their precious energy. If you are viewing responsibly, the eagle shouldn't even know you are there.

Description: This area was farmed in colonial times; until recently it was part of the former Pease Air Force Base. The open fields and oak and pine forests retain reminders of the human presence. Two trails provide access to different habitats: one to Peverly Ponds, the other to the shores of Great Bay.

Viewing Information: The refuge is an excellent place to see and hear wild turkeys throughout the year; they frequent the old roads and have adjusted to being observed. Other wildlife is also plentiful, including white-tailed deer, coyotes, and red and gray foxes. The varied habitat brings neotropical migrants in the spring and summer: rose-breasted grosbeaks, scarlet tanagers, and indigo buntings. From autumn through spring you may see bald eagles, American black ducks, and common loons on the bay.

Directions: *From Interstate 95, take the Spaulding Turnpike west. Drive 3 miles past Portsmouth to the Pease International Tradeport exit in Newington. Follow Merrimack Road, turn right on McIntyre Road, and follow it to the overpass at the entrance to the refuge.*

Ownership: USFWS (603) 431-7511

Size: 1,100 acres   **Closest Town:** Portsmouth

COASTAL

Thanks to restoration efforts begun in the mid-1970s, wild turkey populations are on the rise in New Hampshire. Male turkeys can be heard gobbling on May mornings to attract a hen. GEORGE WUERTHNER

66. SANDY POINT DISCOVERY CENTER

Description: Located on Great Bay, Sandy Point Discovery Center offers inside and outside exhibits and a boardwalk across a tidal marsh. At low tide, more than half of Great Bay is exposed as mudflats. Hearty salt marsh grasses (Spartina) grow along the edges of the bay, helping to create new land and making the water productive for lobsters, flounder, and other sea life.

Viewing Information: Visit during fall shorebird migration to see a variety of sandpipers and plovers, including greater and lesser yellowlegs, killdeer, and spotted, least, and semipalmated sandpipers. You might glimpse some rarer birds too, including dunlins and short-billed dowitchers. In late April and early May, during spring warbler migration, look for northern parulas, black-throated blue warblers, and palm warblers. In the spring and summer, ospreys nest in the area. Waterfowl that winter in the area include common goldeneyes, buffleheads, and common and red-breasted mergansers.

Directions: Take exit 3 off Interstate 95, and head west on Route 33 (formerly Rte. 101) for 5.5 miles. Turn right on Depot Road and follow it to the end.

Ownership: GBNERR (603) 868-1095

Size: 5,300 acres   **Closest Town:** Greenland

67. CHAPMAN'S LANDING

Description: Located on the Squamscott River, Chapman's Landing looks out over salt marsh and tidal flats. The landing provides boat access to Great Bay.

Viewing Information: Here you can get your boat out onto the bay; you can also watch birds, no matter what the season. From Chapman's Landing, watch for ospreys, great blue herons, glossy ibises, and egrets. Look and listen in the marsh for the salt marsh sharp-tailed sparrow. Spring is a good time to spot green-winged teal. In the fall, observe yellowlegs, semipalmated plovers, and least and semipalmated sandpipers. Winter is the time to watch for ducks: greater scaup, common goldeneyes, American black ducks, and mallards all visit the landing.

Directions: Take exit 3 off Interstate 95 and head west on Route 33 (formerly Rte. 101). After 5.6 miles, turn right on Squamscott Road. Chapman's Landing is on the left just before the junction of Squamscott Road and Rte. 108.

Ownership: NHFG; adjacent land under conservation easement to GBNERR (603) 868-1095

Size: 2.4 acres   **Closest Town:** Stratham

68. ODIORNE POINT STATE PARK

Description: Come to Odiorne Point to explore New Hampshire's rocky ocean shore. The park's Seacoast Science Center offers a variety of discovery programs and interpretive exhibits.

Viewing Information: Odiorne Point is a great place to explore tidepools; search for sea stars, mussels, snails, hermit crabs, rock crabs, and an other sea life. *BE EXTREMELY CAREFUL IN THESE AREAS; THE ROCKS ARE VERY SLIPPERY AND SHARP. BE AWARE OF WAVES AND TIDES.* Herring, ring-billed, and black-backed gulls feed along the shore. Watch for double-crested cormorants on the rocks, drying their wings. In the wintertime, see rafts of eiders, scoters, and other sea ducks. During spring and fall migrations, observe shorebirds, warblers, and other songbirds.

Directions: *From the Portsmouth traffic circle, follow the Route 1 Bypass toward "Beaches and Hampton." Drive south 1.9 miles, past Yokens Restaurant. Turn left at the stoplights onto Elwyn Road. Continue for about 1.5 miles to the stop sign at the Foyes Corner intersection with Rte. 1A. Take Rte. 1A south. After 1.1 miles, look for the Odiorne Point State Park north parking area and boat launch on the left. The park's main entrance and the Seacoast Science Center are 0.7 mile farther south.*

Ownership: DRED—Division of Parks and Recreation; Seacoast Science Center is managed by ASNH (603) 436-8043

Size: 332 acres   **Closest Town:** Portsmouth

Adult harbor seals are most active at high tide, generally hauling out to sleep on rocks and rocky ledges at low tide. They eat a variety of fish, shrimp, and shelled animals. JOHN H. GAVIN

69. ISLES OF SHOALS

Description: The Isles of Shoals are 6 miles off the New Hampshire coast. Fewer than half the islands that make up this group are within New Hampshire's borders—Star, Lunging, White Islands, and Square Rock. Star Island, the largest, is 48 acres and is owned by the Unitarian Universalists and the United Church of Christ. You can visit Star Island during the day; make reservations with the Isles of Shoals Steamship Company. A good time to visit is during migration seasons.

Viewing Information: Double-crested cormorants, common eiders, herring and great black-backed gulls, and black guillemots nest on the islands. Visitors to the Shoals can also look for seabirds such as Manx shearwaters, Wilson's storm-petrels, black-legged kittiwakes, dovekies, thick-billed murres, and razorbills. During fall and spring migration, you are likely to see a variety of warblers such as Wilson's, hooded, orange-crowned, mourning, and Cape May.

Directions: *Arrange boat trips to the islands with the Isles of Shoals Steamship Company, Market Street, Portsmouth, NH 03801. Telephone (603) 431-5500 or (800) 441-4620 from outside New Hampshire, (800) 894-5509 from inside the state.*

Ownership: Varies from island to island   **Closest Town:** Portsmouth

70. SEABROOK HARBOR

Description: The Seabrook-Hampton estuary and harbor is an excellent place for year-round birding. The time of year and the tides determine what's on view.

Viewing Information: Seabrook is a reliable place to find migrating and wintering waterfowl such as common loons, common goldeneyes, buffleheads, and common and red-breasted mergansers. Roseate, Forster's, and common terns make appearances in July and August. In August and September, look for black-bellied and semipalmated plovers, killdeer, whimbrels, ruddy turnstones, sanderlings, and several kinds of sandpipers. A variety of gulls visits the area, including Bonaparte's, ring-billed, herring, and great black-backed.

Directions: *From Hampton Beach State Park, continue south on Route 1A for 0.7 mile. Look for the paved parking lot on the west side of Rte. 1A.*

Ownership: Town of Seabrook (603) 474-3311

Size: 1,800 acres   **Closest Town:** Seabrook

71. URBAN FORESTRY CENTER

Description: The Urban Forestry Center, operated by the New Hampshire Division of Forests and Lands, includes a historic house, public meeting facilities, forestry demonstration areas, and a picnic area. Interpretive trails provide access along Sagamore Creek, which is tidal.

Viewing Information: This is a good place to become familiar with year-round resident birds such as downy woodpeckers, black-capped chickadees, white-breasted nuthatches, and house finches. Even though the center is described as urban, you may get a glimpse of red foxes, white-tailed deer, and woodchucks, as well as gray and red squirrels. In summer, look in the saltgrass marsh along Sagamore Creek for great blue herons, black-crowned night herons, and snowy egrets. The oaks, pines, and shrubby vegetation are good places to look for warblers during fall and spring migrations.

Directions: *From Interstate 95, take the exit for Portsmouth traffic circle. From the circle take the Rte. 1 bypass to Route 1 (also called Lafayette Road). Proceed approximately 2 miles through a series of five lights to the stoplights near Yoken's Restuarant. Turn left onto Elwyn Road. In approximately 500 feet take your first left into the Urban Forestry Center.*

Ownership: DRED Division of Forests and Lands (603) 271-3456, or (603) 431-6774

Size: 170 acres   **Closest Town:** Portsmouth

COASTAL

Woodchucks, also referred to as groundhogs, are seen in the spring and summer. They feed voraciously on grasses, roots, stems, and berries to gain the weight necessary to sustain them through six months of hibernation. JOHN H. GAVIN

93

72. PAWTUCKAWAY STATE PARK

Description: There are two ways to access Pawtuckaway State Park. One way provides access to the 800-acre Pawtuckaway Lake and state park facilities, which include a beach, picnic area, and campgrounds. There are several interesting marshes and upland areas to check out when driving from the park entrance to the picnic and camping areas. The other way leads you along marshes and through oak and white pine forest to a lookout tower. The park includes many geologic features, including a boulder field and the Pawtuckaway Mountains, which are part of an eroded volcanic cone.

Viewing Information: The diversity of habitats in the park means there are opportunities to see a variety of wildlife. In the marsh areas look for evidence of beavers, muskrats, otters, and raccoons. Amphibians and turtles are present in large numbers. A variety of songbirds such as common yellowthroats, chestnut-sided warblers, rufous-sided towhees, veeries, hermit thrushes, solitary and red-eyed vireos, and scarlet tanagers are found during the summer months. In recent years, cerulean, worm-eating, and hooded warblers have been sighted. During September and October, the lookout tower provides a good place to view fall hawk migration, while in the summer turkey vultures and common ravens are often seen.

Directions: *Access to the lookout tower is provided from Route 4. From Rte. 4 head south on Rte. 107 for 9.8 miles. Turn left on Reservation Road. At 1 mile the road turns to dirt. Continue another 0.2 mile and bear right at the fork. Continue another 1.2 miles along Reservation Road to a T. At the T turn left. Continue another 0.7 mile to the trailhead parking for the tower. A short trail leads to the tower at 908 feet in elevation. To get to the main park entrance, travel north 1.5 miles on Rte. 156 from its junction with Rte. 27. Turn west and proceed for approximately 2 miles.*

Ownership: DRED Division of Forests and Lands (603) 271-3456 and Division of Parks and Recreation (603) 271-3556

Size: 5,500 acres　　**Closest Town:** Raymond

You may get the best views of wildlife while sitting in your car. A vehicle can conceal you from the animals you want to observe. Many animals are used to cars; they don't seem afraid of them and will often pass right by or even approach.

Description: Owned by Belknap County, this area provides year-round recreational opportunities, including downhill and cross-country skiing, horseback riding, hiking, picnicking, and camping. Trails access the Belknap mountain range. A universally accessible boardwalk leads to a small wetland with wildlife viewing opportunities.

Viewing Information: The area surrounding the wetland and small pond is mixed forest type with maples, red oaks, and white pines. In the summer, a variety of songbirds such as common yellowthroats, red-eyed vireos, veeries, and hermit thrushes can be heard. Great blue herons regularly feed in the pond. Look carefully for evidence of beavers and fishers. Deer are commonly seen and a moose is a possibility.

Directions: From Route 11 in Laconia, turn right onto Rte. 11A heading toward Gilford, follow this to the entrance for Gunstock. Turn right and go approximately 0.4 mile to parking lot access for the boardwalk.

Ownership: Belknap County (603) 528-8713

Size: 5 acres   **Closest Town:** Gilford

COASTAL

Listen for the "witchity, witchity, witchity" of the common yellowthroat along the edges of damp woods, swamps, streams, and ponds. The male has a black mask, and the female has only the rich yellow throat. KEVIN A. BYRON

95

WILDLIFE INDEX

The index below identifies some of the more interesting, uncommon, or attractive wildlife found in New Hampshire, and some of the best sites for viewing selected species. Many of the animals listed may be seen at other sites as well. The numbers following each species are site numbers, rather than page numbers.

Mammals

bears, black: 6, 7, 14, 20

beavers: 12, 17, 18, 24, 29, 32, 33, 36, 39, 42, 43, 57, 58, 62

chipmunks, eastern: 1, 2, 4, 5, 9, 11, 13, 14, 15, 16, 18, 19, 20, 29, 31, 41, 42, 48, 52, 51, 62

coyotes: 2, 8, 10, 13, 22, 23, 34, 47, 50, 53, 65

deer, white-tailed: 1, 2, 3, 4, 5, 7, 8, 12, 13, 22, 23, 24, 27, 30, 33, 34, 36, 39, 40, 46, 49, 48, 50, 53, 54, 62, 64, 63, 65

foxes, red: 13, 22, 23, 27, 34, 46, 50, 51, 62, 64, 63, 65, 68

hares, snowshoe: 2, 14, 15, 16, 17, 19 20, 23, 29, 31, 42

martens, pine: 6

minks: 1, 3, 8, 17, 18, 21, 24, 25, 27, 29, 33, 34, 41, 43, 45, 50, 51, 53, 54, 55, 56, 57, 58, 60, 63, 64

moose: 2, 3, 7, 8, 9, 10, 20, 25, 37

muskrats: 10, 25, 29, 33, 32, 34, 49, 51, 54, 57, 58, 62

otters: 1, 3, 8, 9, 25, 33, 34, 41, 50, 51, 54, 57, 58

seals, harbor: 68, 69

squirrels, gray: 23, 25, 26, 28, 29, 30, 31, 34, 35, 36, 37, 38, 39, 40, 41, 42, 46, 48, 51, 52, 62

squirrels, red: 1, 2, 3, 4, 5, 7, 14, 18, 19, 20, 39

woodchucks: 23, 47, 63

Birds

bluebirds: 13, 22, 23

chickadees, black-capped: 11, 13, 14, 15, 20, 22, 23, 21, 24, 26, 28, 30, 32, 34, 35, 36, 38, 41, 42, 44, 45, 46, 48, 52, 56, 57, 58, 59, 62

chickadees, boreal: 1, 2, 14, 15, 16, 18

cormorants, double-crested: 64, 65, 66, 67, 68, 69, 70

ducks: 3, 8, 10, 24, 25, 27, 29, 33, 34, 35, 42, 46, 49, 50, 51, 53, 54, 57, 58, 60, 63, 64, 65, 66, 67, 68, 69, 70

eagles, bald: 8, 60, 64, 65

egrets: 64, 65, 66, 67, 70

falcons, peregrine: 6, 15, 19

grassland birds: 22, 47, 63, 65

grouse, ruffed: 1, 13, 22, 23, 36, 48

grouse, spruce: 14, 15, 19

gulls: 64, 65, 66, 67, 68, 69, 70

hawks: 11, 31, 52, 60

herons: 8, 10, 33, 35, 54, 64, 66

kingfishers: 1, 9, 27, 41, 46

loons, common: 3, 8, 9, 10, 12, 37, 46

ospreys: 8, 9, 10, 63, 66, 67

ovenbirds: 22, 23, 28, 30, 37, 38, 39, 41, 42, 48, 58

shorebirds: 64, 66, 67, 68, 70

thrushes: 6, 7, 8, 11, 13, 14, 15, 16, 19, 20, 22, 23, 24, 26, 28, 30, 31, 35, 36, 37, 38, 39, 41, 42, 44, 45, 46, 48, 51, 58, 59, 62

turkeys, wild: 34, 54, 65

vireos: 26, 28, 30, 35, 36, 37, 38, 39, 41, 44, 53, 55, 58, 59, 62

warblers: 1, 2, 3, 4, 5, 6, 7, 8, 11, 13, 14, 15, 16, 19, 23, 24, 26, 28, 30, 32

woodcocks: 33, 38, 62

woodpeckers: 1, 2, 13, 22, 26, 30, 32, 41, 58, 62

Fish

fish: 21, 60

Invertebrates

marine: 64, 66, 67, 68, 70

Reptiles and Amphibians

frogs and toads: 24, 25, 26, 29, 32, 39, 45, 49, 57, 58, 61, 62, 65

salamanders: 24, 25, 26, 29, 32, 39, 45, 49, 57, 58, 61, 62, 65

turtles: 24, 29, 39, 43, 57, 58, 62